An

ECCLESIASTICAL CATECHISM

of the

PRESBYTERIAN CHURCH

for the use of

Families, Bible-classes, and Private Members

(Newly revised. Original edition printed in 1843.)

By REV. THOMAS SMYTH, D. D.

(1808-1873)

former pastor of Second Presbyterian Church, Charleston, S.C.

1996 & 2007 editions edited by Rev. Geoffrey W. Donnan

Seventh Edition

ISBN: 0-9773442-3-1

©1996, 2006 Geoffrey W. Donnan

Reformation Christian Ministries
13950 - 122nd Street
Fellsmere, FL 32948-6411 U.S.A.
Phone: 772-571-8833; Fax 772-571-8010
Email: press@reformation.edu
Web Site: http://www.reformation.ws

Scripture quotations are taken from the King James Version.
All Scripture insertions and Greek/Hebrew fonts taken from
BibleWorks for Windows™ by Hermeneutika.™

Cover:
Cover drawing of Westminster Cathedral in London, England. The Westminster Assembly met here, initially from July 1, 1643 in the Henry VII Chapel until the colder weather of the autumn of that year when they moved to the Jerusalem Chamber. It concluded its business on February 22, 1649 drafting many documents collectively known as the Westminster Standards. These became the formal foundation of churches known as Presbyterian churches, though many other denominations utilize that polity without taking that name. This drawing was made by Kimarie Anne Card (nee Donnan) for the first republishing of this document in 1996.

Table of Contents

Original Preface

The necessity for some such work as the present has been long felt by many. Great detriment has accrued to the Presbyterian church, from the want of that indoctrination in the principles of her worship and polity, which it is surely her duty to provide for all, who commit themselves and their offspring to her teaching and guidance. Her members and children have been attached to her, not so much by those ties of principle and conviction, which prove firm and enduring, as by merely local and personal considerations, which form, in times of difficulty, but a feeble bond of attachment. Other churches are diligent in their efforts to imbue the young mind with the knowledge of all their doctrinal peculiarities; and if this is done in a spirit of charity and Christian brotherhood, will it not promote, rather than prevent, that perfect *Christian* union for which we hope?

That this work, which was drawn up at the suggestion of some leading members of our church, is altogether what is needed, the author can hardly dare to hope. He would still offer it as an *attempt*, and not as a full *accomplishment,* of all that he believes to be demanded by the necessities of the church. He has used every effort to procure hints from competent individuals, and would return his thanks to those brethren and gentlemen, who have favored him with their views. Of these he has availed himself, in rendering the work more correct; while, by the sub-division of the chapters, the various topics will, he trusts, be better understood, and more easily comprehended by the learner. To the Rev. Samuel Miller, D.D.[1], the author would especially render thanks, for his kindness in first imposing upon him the preparation of this volume; for his careful revision of it; and for his valuable suggestions.

He has endeavored to render it as full and comprehensive as possible; and, for this purpose, he has availed himself freely of the labors of others. He would particularly refer to the *Ecclesiastical Catechisms* of Dr. McLeod,[2] of the Rev. Samuel Palmer, of one published in Ireland, and of *A Sequel to the Shorter Catechism*, as sources from which he has derived assistance.

It was thought better to err on the side of prolixity, than of brevity[3]; as it was one object of the author to fit the work for private reading, and to make it as satisfactory as possible, on all the leading subjects embraced in its design. The teacher can use his discretion in prescribing to his pupils, whether in the family, the Bible-class, or the Sabbath school, such portions of it as he may deem most necessary to be committed to memory. Other portions he may think it sufficient

---

[1] Samuel Miller (1769-1850) served as a Presbyterian pastor in New York City for over twenty years. In 1813, Miller was selected as the second Professor at Princeton Seminary. For over thirty-five years, he labored there as the Professor of Ecclesiastical history and Church Government. [Ed.]

[2] Dr. Alexander McLeod (died 1833) was pastor of Chamber Street Reformed Presbyterian Church in New York City, New York. his *Ecclesiastical Catechism* was first published in 1806 and republished in 1868. [Ed.]

[3] too long rather than too short [Ed.]

to read with them, accompanied with his own further explanations; and whenever he may think any answer of too great length to be retained in the memory, he may, after such reading and examination, require it to be given in substance, in the language of the pupil.

Although the author has heard of but one opinion as to the usefulness of the work, yet, when he found that the second edition was entirely exhausted, he carefully revised the whole, altered and remodeled several portions, and added some sections, (as on the apostolic succession, and the relation of the Presbyterian church to the world,) which will, it is hoped, increase the usefulness of the work.

In the fervent hope that it may lead some of the rising generation to ask for the old paths, that they may walk therein, it is committed to the blessing of the Head of the church, by his most unworthy servant.

Charleston, South Carolina, 1843 — Thomas Smyth.

Preface from the Editor

This edition is based upon the 3rd Edition published in 1843 in New York by Leavitt & Trow.

As much as possible for accuracy, this text was left in its original wording. Some words have been changed when it was determined that they were too misleading or archaic (e.g., *looks* replaces *looketh, Spirit* replaces *Ghost*). Where additions have been made by the editor to the text for understanding, this was done by placing the addition in brackets [ ] or noted by placing [Ed.] after the addition, in the case of lengthier additions which are generally footnoted. Punctuation and capitalization have been made consistent with modern rules except in original quotations. This edition is something of a working draft, therefore, your comments or corrections are solicited to the publisher's address.

Westminster Confession of Faith references are first given in the original 1647 edition with U.S. edition citations in parentheses following.

Special thanks is given to Rev. Mark Brown and Dr. Jeffrey Boer for their encouragement and assistance in the republication of this catechism. Additional gratitude is expressed to Deborah Vanden Heuvel and George and Cynthia Molenaar for their assistance in typing and editing this manuscript.

It is hoped that you and your church and most of all, the church of Jesus Christ, will grow in maturity and knowledge by the republication of this great work.

Fellsmere, Florida, 2007 — Geoffrey W. Donnan

CHAPTER 1
OF THE CHURCH

Section 1
The different meanings of the word "church", as used in Scripture.[4]

1.   *What is the meaning of the term "church", as used in Scripture?*

The word *church*, as used in Scripture, has various significations, being used both in a common and a sacred sense.

2.   *What is the meaning of the word "church", as used in Scripture in a common sense?*

The word, which is translated *church*, is used in Scripture in the common sense, to signify any public assembly of persons to consult together.

Acts 19: 32, 39, 41 — Some therefore cried one thing, and some another: for the assembly was confused; and the more part knew not wherefore they were come together... But if ye enquire any thing concerning other matters, it shall be determined in a lawful assembly... And when he had thus spoken, he dismissed the assembly.

3.   *What is the sacred sense, in which the word "church" is most generally used in Scripture?[5]*

This word is, in its sacred sense, applied to the church of Christ, which is a society of men called of God, by the Gospel, unto the faith and worship of the Lord Jesus Christ, and of God in him.

4.   *What is the first meaning of the word "church" in this sacred sense?*

It means any particular congregation or society of professing Christians.

Colossians 4:15 — Salute the brethren which are in Laodicea, and Nymphas, and the church which is in his house.
Romans 16:5 — Likewise *greet* the church that is in their house. Salute my well beloved Epaenetus, who is the firstfruits of Achaia unto Christ.

---

[4]   See valuable work on the Bib. Repertory, April, 1845, p. 218 and 226, and also for July, 1845. Act. on Genesis Assembly on Romish Baptism. Stillingfleet's *Protestant Religion*, p. 46 and p. 50.

[5]   *Ecclesia* was used by the writers of the Septuagint version, which was familiar to the New Testament writers, for the word *congregation,* as it stands in our version of the Old Testament. It is on this account that in the New Testament instead of the word *congregation,* we have *church,* which is the same as *kirk* or *assembly.*

5. *What is the second meaning of the word "church" in this sacred sense?*

It is applied to several congregations, or churches, considered as one body[6], under the same general superintendence.

1 Corinthians 1:2 — Unto the church of God which is at Corinth, to them that are sanctified in Christ Jesus, called *to be* saints, with all that in every place call upon the name of Jesus Christ our Lord, both theirs and ours:

1 Corinthians 14:34 — Let your women keep silence in the churches: for it is not permitted unto them to speak; but *they are commanded* to be under obedience, as also saith the law.

Acts 8:1 — And Saul was consenting unto his death. And at that time there was a great persecution against the church which was at Jerusalem; and they were all scattered abroad throughout the regions of Judaea and Samaria, except the apostles.

Acts 21:20 — And when they heard *it*, they glorified the Lord, and said unto him, Thou seest, brother, how many thousands of Jews there are which believe; and they are all zealous of the law:

6. *What is the third meaning of the word "church" in its sacred sense?*

It means any assembly of the rulers of the church when convened as an ecclesiastical judicatory [court]. [7]

Matthew 18:15-17 — Moreover if your brother sins against you, go and tell him his fault between you and him alone. If he hears you, you have gained your brother. But if he will not hear, take with you one or two more, that "by the mouth of two or three witnesses every word may be established." And if he refuses to hear them, tell it to the church. But if he refuses even to hear the church, let him be to you like a heathen and a tax collector.

Hebrews 13:17 — Obey those who rule over you, and be submissive, for they watch out for your souls, as those who must give account. Let them do so with joy and not with grief, for that would be unprofitable for you.

See also Acts 14:27; Acts 15:2, 30, 22; Acts 11:26; 1 Corinthians 5. [8]

Section 2
The distinction between the church, as visible and invisible. [9]

7. *What is the fourth meaning of the word "church" in its sacred sense?*

It means the whole body of God's redeemed people, that have been, or shall be, gathered into one, under Christ the Head, and which is generally called *the invisible church.* *(cont'd)*

---

[6] Often referred to today by the word *denomination*. [Ed.]

[7] That the word *church* means *an assembly of rulers meeting together in an ecclesiastical judicatory* [court], see largely proved in Dr. Ayton's *Original Constitution of the Church*, ch. ii, 3, pp. 63,64. Brown's *Dictionary of the Bible*, Art. Church. Livingstone's *Theology*, p. 261.

[8] That this meaning is to be attached to the term *church* in these places, and that it is in itself an important meaning, was maintained by the early writers in defense of Presbyterianism. I may refer particularly to Rutherford's *Due Right of Presbyteries*, &c. 4 to. London, 1644, at pp. 309, 314, 322, 489-491. See also pp. 316, 348. See also his plea for Paul's Presbyteries [*A Peaceable and Temperate Plea for Paul's Presbyteries in Scotland*...ed.], 4 to. London, 1642, p. 85, &c. Gillespie's *Aaron's Rod Blossoming*, 4 to. London, 1646, pp. 294-297, and 350-467. See further, *Jus Divinum Regiminis Ecclesiastici* [*The Divine Right of Church Government*, Napthali Press; available through Reformation Media and Press, ed.], by the London Ministers, 4 to. London, 1654, p. 208, &c. See also many authorities produced in Paget's *Definition of Presbyterian Church Government*. London, 1641, pp. 50, 51.

[9] See *Biblical Repertory*, April 1845, p. 223.

Ephesians 5:25-27 — Husbands, love your wives, even as Christ also loved the church, and gave himself for it; That he might sanctify and cleanse it with the washing of water by the word, That he might present it to himself a glorious church, not having spot, or wrinkle, or any such thing; but that it should be holy and without blemish.

Colossians 1:18 — And he is the head of the body, the church: who is the beginning, the firstborn from the dead; that in all *things* he might have the preeminence.

See also Ephesians 1:10, 22, 23; Hebrews 12:23.

8. *Why is the church called invisible?*

Because its union with Christ is a spiritual union; because the faith and love of those who are its true members are invisible to men, and infallibly discerned only by God, who looks upon the heart; and because, in this sense, the church has no visible or formal existence on earth, but is an object of faith, being composed of all Christ's faithful members, wherever they are found.

9. *What is the fifth meaning of the word "church" in its sacred sense?*

It means the whole body of those, throughout the world, of every denomination, with their children, who profess the true religion, and which is commonly called *the visible church*.

Acts 2:39, 47 — For the promise is unto you, and to your children, and to all that are afar off, *even* as many as the Lord our God shall call…Praising God, and having favour with all the people. And the Lord added to the church daily such as should be saved.

1 Corinthians 12:12, 13, 28 — or as the body is one, and hath many members, and all the members of that one body, being many, are one body: so also *is* Christ. For by one Spirit are we all baptized into one body, whether *we be* Jews or Gentiles, whether *we be* bond or free; and have been all made to drink into one Spirit… And God hath set some in the church, first apostles, secondarily prophets, thirdly teachers, after that miracles, then gifts of healings, helps, governments, diversities of tongues.

1 Corinthians 15:9 — For I am the least of the apostles, that am not meet to be called an apostle, because I persecuted the church of God.

Acts 8 [esp. v. 3, ed.] — As for Saul, he made havock of the church, entering into every house, and haling men and women committed *them* to prison.

1 Corinthians 10:32 — Give none offence, neither to the Jews, nor to the Gentiles, nor to the church of God:

10. *Why is the church, in this sense, called the visible church?*

Because all are members of it who make a profession of the Christian religion, including those who, while they are members of the church on earth, may not be members of the church invisible, nor possessed of either faith or love.

11. *May there, then, be distinct branches or sections of the visible church?*

Yes; there may be distinct branches or sections of the visible church existing in different kingdoms, as the Church of Scotland, the Church of Geneva, the Church of England, & c.[10,11] These all, so far as they hold the same faith, are component parts of the one universal visible church; in the same manner as the waters of the different

---

[10] "*& c*" is an abbreviation meaning *and so forth.*

[11] At the time this was written, the major churches in other nations were often still strongly state churches, many of which have now considerably apostacized from the faith as bodies, though there are often notable individuals and churches within them which are exceptions.

seas, however variously distributed and called, are nevertheless connected among themselves, and form component parts of one and the
same great ocean.

12.   *Does this distinction of the church into visible and invisible make two
churches instead of one?*

It does not; since by these terms we only distinguish the church in its
external form, from the same church in its internal or spiritual character. As visible, it includes hypocrites; as invisible, only believers.
As visible, it requires from its members only an external and credible
profession of the faith; as invisible, it supposes in every member a
sincere and hearty reception of the truth, in the love of it.[12]

13.   *To which of these churches are left the promises of perpetuity and
indefectibility?*

Not to the visible church, which may fail and err in any of its parts,
but to the invisible, against which the gates of hell cannot prevail,
and with which Christ will be, even to the end of the world. So that
there shall always be those, somewhere, who shall believe and profess
the true religion.

Section 3
The present use of the word "church" in these several senses.

14.   *Is the word "church" still commonly used in these various senses?*

Yes, in all of them except the common sense, in which it is not used,
because it is now exclusively applied to religious bodies and in its
sacred sense.

15.   *Can you give me an illustration of the use of the word "church" in the
first meaning?*

We speak of the several churches in any town or city, and also, when
there are more than one of the same denomination, as, for instance,
the Presbyterian, we speak of the first, second, or third Presbyterian
church.

---

[12] See this meaning of the word fully developed in Hooker, *Ecclesiastical Polity,* book 3, sec. 1, in
Works, vol. i. p. 195, Hanbury's edition, London, 1830, 3 vols. 8 vo. See also p. 255. See also
Bishop Hopkin's *Works,* vol. ii. p. 418. This subject may also be seen fully discussed in Roger's
Discourse and Review of the Visible and Invisible Church of Christ. London, 1721. Dr. George
Miller, in his recent letter to Dr. Pusey, London, 1840, at p. 22, speaks of the fundamental error or
rejecting the distinction between the visible and the invisible church of Christ. See also pp. 23-25,
where he calls this distinction *the essential principle of the Reformation, and very plainly
discoverable in the articles (that is, the Thirty-Nine Articles) of our church'"* See also *Essays on
the Church,* Introductory, p. 5, &c. Nolans's *Catholic Character of Christ,* p. 73. *The Church in
the World,* pp. 54, 79. Neander's *Plant of the Christian Church,* vol. ii. pp. 177, 178, 248. Dr.
Owen's *Works,* vol. xix. pp 152, 167, 209, 215, and authorities on pp. 156, 169. See also the
martyr Philpot's testimony in *London Christian Observer,* 1841, p. 339, and Churchman's
Monthly Review, Dec. 1841, p. 661, where are quoted archbishops Seeker and Hooker.

16. *Can you give me an illustration of the use of the word "church" in the second meaning?*

We speak of the Presbyterian Church in the United States of America[13], and so of other churches.

17. *Can you give me an illustration of the use of the word "church" in the third meaning?*

When the session[14] of a church is assembled together, we say there is a meeting of the church; and when any member has been disciplined or received by that body, we say he has been disciplined or received by that church of which it is the session.

Section 4
Of the church catholic.

18. *What other term is applied to the church of Christ, considered as a whole, besides the terms visible and invisible?*

The term *catholic.*

19. *What is the meaning of the word "catholic"?*

The word *catholic* means universal.

20. *Why is the church of Christ called catholic or universal?*

Because it is not confined to one nation, as it was under the Jewish economy[15], but consists of all those in every part of the world who believe in Christ; because its privileges are conferred equally upon all classes of men; and because it will yet embrace within it all nations and kindreds[16] of the earth.

1 Corinthians 12:12, 13 — For as the body is one, and hath many members, and all the members of that one body, being many, are one body: so also *is* Christ. For by one Spirit are we all baptized into one body, whether *we be* Jews or Gentiles, whether *we be* bond or free; and have been all made to drink into one Spirit.
Psalm 2:8 — Ask of me, and I shall give *thee* the heathen *for* thine inheritance, and the uttermost parts of the earth *for* thy possession.
See also Romans 15:9-12.

21. *What other sense was attached by the early fathers to the word "catholic"?*

It was used by them as synonymous with the term *orthodox*, so that, in this view of it, the true church is to be known by that true doctrine which is everywhere to be preached and to be held fast.

---

[13] This was written in 1843 and the author belonged to this church body (denomination). You may wish to substitute the denomination to which you belong in this answer. [Ed.]

[14] see Chap. 4, sec. 2

[15] i.e. during the Old Testament times [Ed.]

[16] i.e. peoples, tribes, kinds of people [Ed.]

22.   *Has this catholic visible church been perpetuated and preserved?*

Yes; there has always been a visible church catholic which, though divided by place, forms, and names, may yet be considered as one body, holding [to] the Head and professing in substance the true religion.

23.   *In what sense, then, may the visible church be properly said to be catholic or universal?*

The visible church may be properly said to be catholic or universal, not as consisting of one society, under one government, but, as its various societies and churches are, or ought to be, modeled on the same principles; enjoying common privileges, and having one divine Head, even Christ, who rules and guides it by his word and Spirit.

Section 5
Of the unity of the church.

24.   *What do you mean by the unity of the church?*

By the unity of the church, I understand that as there is but one God and Saviour, so all who believe and obey the Gospel are equally adopted into the family of heaven; equally enjoy all the promised blessings of salvation; are equally entitled to the free use of all the means of grace; are baptized into one faith; and are called, justified, and sanctified through the same plan of redeeming love and mercy.

25.   *Is it not further necessary to the unity of the church, that it should be under one earthly head?*

No; there is no other Head of the church than the Lord Jesus Christ, whose house and family it is.

Ephesians 1:23 — Which is his body, the fulness of him that filleth all in all.

26.   *Is it not further necessary to the unity of the church universal, that it should be under the same forms and regulations?*

No; it is only necessary that whatever forms and regulations are adopted by any church, they should be authorized by the word of God, and not contrary to it.

Romans 14:19 — Let us therefore follow after the things which make for peace, and things wherewith one may edify another.
1 Corinthians 14:14, 40 — For if I pray in an *unknown* tongue, my spirit prayeth, but my understanding is unfruitful… Let all things be done decently and in order.
See also Galatians 5:1.

27.   *Is it not further necessary to the unity of the church, that it should, in all things, be governed by one and the same ecclesiastical authority?*

Certainly not! for we read in Scripture of the church at Antioch, the church at Jerusalem, the church at Corinth, the church at Ephesus, the churches of Syria, the churches of Asia; — and in primitive times, there was the Eastern church, the Western, the African, the British, and so on, and these were all separate and distinct.

28. *In what, then, does the unity of the church essentially consist?*

The unity of the church essentially consists in unity of faith, by which all its members hold the same divine truths; and in unity of spirit, or that oneness which subsists between Christ, its Head, and all its members, whereby the same Spirit dwells in all, and works in all the same Christian graces.

Ephesians 4:3, 13 — Endeavouring to keep the unity of the Spirit in the bond of peace...Till we all come in the unity of the faith, and of the knowledge of the Son of God, unto a perfect man, unto the measure of the stature of the fulness of Christ:
See also 2 Corinthians 11:4; Jude 3; Galatians 1:8, 9; 1 Peter 5:9; Colossians 1:2, 7, 23.

Section 6
Of pure, imperfect, corrupt, and false churches.

29. *Are we, then, to understand that all particular churches[17] are equally churches of Christ?*

All particular churches which agree in holding the truth as it is in Jesus; which profess sound doctrine; which maintain the preaching of the word, and administration of the sacraments; and which thus hold the truth in love, are justly distinguished by the name and authority of true visible churches. Nevertheless, all true churches are not perfect, neither are all churches true churches, but some are corrupt and some false.

30. *Is it not, then necessary to distinguish between the nature and essence of a church, and the integrity and perfection of a church? and what is that distinction?*

The nature and essence of [a] church, consists in the preaching of the pure word of God, and the due administration of sacraments, so that where these are, there is a visible church. The integrity or perfection of a church consists, further, in that apostolic form, order, and ministry, which can be traced to the institution of Christ and his apostles.

31. *What, then, do you mean by a pure church?[18]*

By a pure church, or portion of the visible church, I mean a society whose confession of faith agrees with the doctrine of Jesus Christ and his apostles; and which is governed solely by the laws laid down in the word of God, or drawn from it by plain and necessary inference.

32. *What, then, are the signs of a pure church?*

The signs of a pure church are soundness of doctrine, a lawful and regular ministry, the prevalence of love among its members and

---

[17] *Particular churches* refers to individual congregations or churches [Ed.].

[18] *Biblical Repertory*, April, 1845, p. 231, and Stillingfleet's *Protestant Religion*, p. 503. 29, VOL. IV

towards all saints, and the due administration of Gospel ordinances, including discipline.

Ephesians 2:20 — And are built upon the foundation of the apostles and prophets, Jesus Christ himself being the chief corner *stone*;
Acts 2:42 — And they continued stedfastly in the apostles' doctrine and fellowship, and in breaking of bread, and in prayers.
Acts 14:23 — And when they had ordained them elders in every church, and had prayed with fasting, they commended them to the Lord, on whom they believed.
Matthew 28:19 — Go ye therefore, and teach all nations, baptizing them in the name of the Father, and of the Son, and of the Holy Ghost:
See also Acts 20:7.

33.   *Is not antiquity as it regards its visible form, one mark of a pure church?*

It is not; since, judged by this standard, the Jewish would be the only true church; while other forms of religion also lay claims to greater antiquity than the Christian. Besides, the signs of all true churches being those laid down in the Bible must, therefore, be as ancient as Christianity itself.

34.   *Is not universality, in the extent of its authority and government, the mark of a pure church?*

Universality, in the sense of universal extent, is not a mark of a pure church; for no church is, or ever has been, in this sense, universal; and the assumptions of any such authority, by any one church, over all others, is antichristian usurpation.

35.   *Is the possession of a clear and uninterrupted personal succession in its ministers, from the time of the apostles, the necessary mark of a pure church?*

Such a personal succession cannot be the mark of a pure church, because it cannot be shown by any church on earth; because, if it had been essential, such a succession would have been preserved free from doubt or interruption; because it is nowhere laid down in the Scriptures; and because the Scriptures show that even when an unquestioned succession did exist, God withdrew his presence and forsook the apostate church.[19]

Jeremiah 7:4 — Trust ye not in lying words, saying, The temple of the LORD, The temple of the LORD, The temple of the LORD, *are* these.
Malachi 2:1, 9 — And now, O ye priests, this commandment *is* for you... Therefore have I also made you contemptible and base before all the people, according as ye have not kept my ways, but have been partial in the law.
Romans 9:6-8 — Not as though the word of God hath taken none effect. For they *are* not all Israel, which are of Israel: Neither, because they are the seed of Abraham, *are they* all children: but, In Isaac shall thy seed be called. That is, They which are the children of the flesh, these *are* not the children of God: but the children of the promise are counted for the seed.

---

[19] See chapter vii. sect. v. for a full consideration of this subject.

36. *What do you mean by an imperfect church?*

By an imperfect church I understand a church which continues steadfastly in the apostles' doctrine, teaching the pure word of God, and omitting no essential truth of the Gospel; but which, at the same time, has not the sacraments duly administered, nor its order, polity, and ministry perfectly conformed to the scriptural model.

37. *What do you mean by a corrupt church?*

By a corrupt church I understand one which, while it preserves the essential truths of the Gospel, at the same time adds other things to these truths which are not found in God's word, or are repugnant to the same; and which thus, by human traditions or any other spurious authority, makes vain the preaching of the truth and corrupts the administration of divine ordinances.[20]

38. *What do you mean by a false church?*

That church which has laid any other foundation than Christ and his righteousness; which has denied any of the essential doctrines of the word of God; or interpreted the word of God according to its own vain imagination; such a church, whatever else it may possess of order or discipline, and however it may claim the temple, the priesthood, antiquity, or succession — is a false church.

Revelation 2:9 — I know thy works, and tribulation, and poverty, (but thou art rich) and *I know* the blasphemy of them which say they are Jews, and are not, but *are* the synagogue of Satan.

39. *What, then, would you say of each of these churches?*

All churches which are imperfect, ought to be improved; such as are corrupt, reformed; while such as are false, ought to be defeated,[21] and their foundations laid again.

40. *May there, then, be true Christians within the bosom of false and apostate churches?*

We are certainly taught that within such churches there may be some who are true Christians, and therefore members of the invisible church; and who, with more or less publicity, bear testimony against their error. But as they are in great danger, we are to invite all who are members of such churches to come out from among them, and be separate, and touch not the unclean thing.

1 Kings 19:18 — Yet I have left *me* seven thousand in Israel, all the knees which have not bowed unto Baal, and every mouth which hath not kissed him.
Isaiah 1:9 — Except the LORD of hosts had left unto us a very small remnant, we should have been as Sodom, *and* we should have been like unto Gomorrah.
Romans 11:28 — As concerning the gospel, *they are* enemies for your sakes: but as touching the election, *they are* beloved for the fathers' sakes.   *(cont'd)*

---

[20] i.e., the Lord's Supper and baptism [Ed.].
[21] Original, *subverted* [Ed.]

Isaiah 10:20, 22 — And it shall come to pass in that day, *that* the remnant of Israel, and such as are escaped of the house of Jacob, shall no more again stay upon him that smote them; but shall stay upon the LORD, the Holy One of Israel, in truth... For though thy people Israel be as the sand of the sea, *yet* a remnant of them shall return: the consumption decreed shall overflow with righteousness.
See also Ezekiel 9:4; 2 Peter 2:8; Psalm 119:53, 136; Revelation 12:6, 14; Acts 9:31; Revelation 18:4.

Section 7
Of the perpetuity and necessity of the church.

41. *Are we, then, to believe in the perpetuity of the church of Christ?*

Our Saviour has declared that the church is built upon a rock; that the gates of Hades[22] shall not prevail against it; and that He will be with it always, even to end of the world.

Matthew 16:18 — And I say also unto thee, That thou art Peter, and upon this rock I will build my church; and the gates of hell[23] shall not prevail against it.
Matthew 28:20 — Teaching them to observe all things whatsoever I have commanded you: and, lo, I am with you alway, *even* unto the end of the world. Amen.
See also Isaiah 59:21; Acts 2:47; Titus 2:14; 1 Peter 2:9.10; Isaiah 61:8, 9; Daniel 2:14, 44; John 14:14, 16, 17; 1 Thessalonians 4:18; Matthew 13:41-49; Ephesians 4:11-13.

42. *Does a full belief in the certain perpetuity of the church of Christ imply a belief in the perpetuity of any particular visible church?*

There is nothing in the word of God to warrant a belief in the perpetuity, or continued purity, of any particular visible church. On the contrary, we are there admonished that even apostolic churches had fallen away, and would finally become extinct; and that a very general corruption of the Gospel, which had then commenced, would be consummated, to the destruction of many souls.

Revelation 2:5, 16, 24 — Remember therefore from whence thou art fallen, and repent, and do the first works; or else I will come unto thee quickly, and will remove thy candlestick out of his place, except thou repent... Repent; or else I will come unto thee quickly, and will fight against them with the sword of my mouth... But unto you I say, and unto the rest in Thyatira, as many as have not this doctrine, and which have not known the depths of Satan, as they speak; I will put upon you none other burden.
See also Revelation 3:3, 4, 15, 16.
Revelation 18:2 — And he cried mightily with a strong voice, saying, Babylon the great is fallen, is fallen, and is become the habitation of devils, and the hold of every foul spirit, and a cage of every unclean and hateful bird.
See also 2 Thessalonians 2:11, 12; 1 Timothy 4:1, 6; 2 Timothy 3:13; 2 Peter 3:1, 3; Revelation 17:10; Acts 20:30; 1 John 2:19; 2 John 7; Jude 18.
Romans 11:18, 22 — Boast not against the branches. But if thou boast, thou bearest not the root, but the root thee... Behold therefore the goodness and severity of God: on them which fell, severity; but toward thee, goodness, if thou continue in *his* goodness: otherwise thou also shalt be cut off.
See also 1 John 2:1, 4.

---

[22] Original, *hell* [Ed.]
[23] literally *hades* [Ed.]

43. *Is a connection with any visible church sufficient to secure the salvation of the soul?*

On the contrary, our connection with a false church may lead to the damnation of the soul by involving it in the guilt of its heresies and abominations. Neither is salvation to be secured in any other way than by believing in the Lord Jesus Christ as the only propitiation for sins.

2 Thessalonians 2:11, 12 — And for this cause God shall send them strong delusion, that they should believe a lie: That they all might be damned who believed not the truth, but had pleasure in unrighteousness.
2 Peter 2:1-3 — But there were false prophets also among the people, even as there shall be false teachers among you, who privily shall bring in damnable heresies, even denying the Lord that bought them, and bring upon themselves swift destruction. And many shall follow their pernicious ways; by reason of whom the way of truth shall be evil spoken of. And through covetousness shall they with feigned words make merchandise of you: whose judgment now of a long time lingereth not, and their damnation slumbereth not.
See also Matthew 24:5,11, 24.
1 Timothy 4:1 — Now the Spirit speaketh expressly, that in the latter times some shall depart from the faith, giving heed to seducing spirits, and doctrines of devils;
See also Acts 7:42.
1 Corinthians 11:19 — For there must be also heresies among you, that they which are approved may be made manifest among you.
See also 2 Timothy 3:1, 15; Romans 2:25, 29; Galatians 5:6; John 3.

44. *What, then, are we to understand by the doctrine that out of the church there is no ordinary possibility of salvation?*

By this doctrine we are to understand that faith, and consequently salvation, are ordinarily bestowed by God through the instrumentality of his ministers, and that it is only in this way that men are ordinarily introduced into the invisible church, out of which there is no salvation. But it does not teach, that salvation cannot be obtained out of any particular visible Church, by whatever name it may be called; neither is such a claim, on the part of any church, to be otherwise regarded than as both impious and vain.

Colossians 1:18 — And he is the head of the body, the church: who is the beginning, the firstborn from the dead; that in all *things* he might have the preeminence.
Ephesians 5:23 — For the husband is the head of the wife, even as Christ is the head of the church: and he is the saviour of the body.
See also Romans 10:14, 15.
1 Corinthians 5:12, 13 — For what have I to do to judge them also that are without? do not ye judge them that are within? But them that are without God judgeth. Therefore put away from among yourselves that wicked person.
Acts 2:47 — Praising God, and having favour with all the people. And the Lord added to the church daily such as should be saved.
Revelation 3:7 — And to the angel of the church in Philadelphia write; These things saith he that is holy, he that is true, he that hath the key of David, he that openeth, and no man shutteth; and shutteth, and no man openeth; *See also Revelation 1:18.*
Romans 5:1, 2, 8 — Therefore being justified by faith, we have peace with God through our Lord Jesus Christ: By whom also we have access by faith into this grace wherein we stand, and rejoice in hope of the glory of God....But God commendeth his love toward us, in that, while we were yet sinners, Christ died for us.
Numbers 23:8 — How shall I curse, whom God hath not cursed? or how shall I defy, *whom* the LORD hath not defied?

45.   *May we expect to find any church, on earth, perfectly free from error?*

The purest existing churches are subject both to mixture and error; and therefore, we must not expect in them absolute perfection.

1 Corinthians 13:12 — For now we see through a glass, darkly; but then face to face: now I know in part; but then shall I know even as also I am known.
Matthew 13:24, 47 — Another parable put he forth unto them, saying, The kingdom of heaven is likened unto a man which sowed good seed in his field:…Again, the kingdom of heaven is like unto a net, that was cast into the sea, and gathered of every kind:
See also Revelation 2 and 3.

46.   *Is it, then, a matter of indifference to what church we belong?*

No; it is our solemn duty to understand the character and signs of a true church of Christ; and to adhere to that church which is found most consonant to the Scriptures, in its doctrines, its ordinances, and its constitution.

Matthew 5:19 — Whosoever therefore shall break one of these least commandments, and shall teach men so, he shall be called the least in the kingdom of heaven: but whosoever shall do and teach *them*, the same shall be called great in the kingdom of heaven.
1 John 4:1 — Beloved, believe not every spirit, but try the spirits whether they are of God: because many false prophets are gone out into the world.
1 Thessalonians 5:21 — Prove all things; hold fast that which is good.

Section 8
Of the duty of different churches;
and of the church militant and triumphant.

47.   *In view of this liability to err, what is the duty of each church?*

It is the duty of every denomination, or church, to reform abuses where they may exist; to endeavor after full conformity to the plan of church order appointed by Christ; to contend earnestly for the faith once delivered to the saints; and to exercise strict discipline over all offenders according to the spiritual laws of Christ's kingdom.

Revelation 2:14, 15 — But I have a few things against thee, because thou hast there them that hold the doctrine of Balaam, who taught Balac to cast a stumblingblock before the children of Israel, to eat things sacrificed unto idols, and to commit fornication. So hast thou also them that hold the doctrine of the Nicolaitans, which thing I hate.

48.   *What is the further duty of the members of each particular church, towards those of every other denomination?*

It is their duty to pray for them; to exercise charity towards them; to live peaceably with them; to remember that to their own master they must give account; while rejoicing in the truth, to hold it in love; and, as far as no sanction is given to error in doctrine or practice, to cooperate with them in every good word and work.

Psalm 122:6 — Pray for the peace of Jerusalem: they shall prosper that love thee.
Romans 14:4 — Who art thou that judgest another man's servant? to his own master he standeth or falleth. Yea, he shall be holden up: for God is able to make him stand.
Romans 12:18 — If it be possible, as much as lieth in you, live peaceably with all men.
1 Corinthians 9:22 — To the weak became I as weak, that I might gain the weak: I am made all things to all *men*, that I might by all means save some.   *(cont'd)*

Galatians 6:10 — To the weak became I as weak, that I might gain the weak: I am made all things to all *men*, that I might by all means save some.
See also 1 Corinthians 13; Jude 3.

49.   **What further division of the church does this consideration of its present division lead you to mention?**

The church is further divided into the *church militant* and the *church triumphant.*

50.   **What is meant by the church militant?**

By the *church militant,* is meant the whole body of true believers in this present evil world; who are called and required of God to contend with many internal and external sufferings, adversities, persecutions, heresies, and temptations.

2 Timothy 4:7 — I have fought a good fight, I have finished *my* course, I have kept the faith:

51.   **What is meant by the church triumphant?**

By the *church triumphant,* is meant the whole number of the elect, the church of the First Born, whose names are written in heaven; who are freed from all temptations and trials; admitted to the most perfect rest and blessedness; and gathered together into one glorious church under Christ their Head.

Ephesians 1:10, 22, 23 — That in the dispensation of the fulness of times he might gather together in one all things in Christ, both which are in heaven, and which are on earth; *even* in him:…And hath put all *things* under his feet, and gave him *to be* the head over all *things* to the church, Which is his body, the fulness of him that filleth all in all.
Hebrews 12:22-24 — But ye are come unto mount Sion, and unto the city of the living God, the heavenly Jerusalem, and to an innumerable company of angels, To the general assembly and church of the firstborn, which are written in heaven, and to God the Judge of all, and to the spirits of just men made perfect, And to Jesus the mediator of the new covenant, and to the blood of sprinkling, that speaketh better things than *that of* Abel.
See also Revelation 21 and 22.

52.   **Should not the hope of this blessed state be shed abroad in all true Christian minds the spirit of kindness and brotherly love?**

Yes. However differing as to their modes of thinking, and their particular opinions and forms; and however divided into particular communions; all real Christians, who hold the Head, ought to regard themselves as constituting but one church, and so to live together in unity of spirit and in the bonds of peace; looking for the blessed hope and the glorious appearing of their common God and Saviour Jesus Christ.

John 13:34 — A new commandment I give unto you, That ye love one another; as I have loved you, that ye also love one another.
Titus 3:3-5 — For we ourselves also were sometimes foolish, disobedient, deceived, serving divers lusts and pleasures, living in malice and envy, hateful, *and* hating one another. But after that the kindness and love of God our Saviour toward man appeared, Not by works of righteousness which we have done, but according to his mercy he saved us, by the washing of regeneration, and renewing of the Holy Ghost;

CHAPTER 2
GOVERNMENT OF THE CHURCH

Section 1
Of church government in general.

53. *What is meant by government?*

Government, in its general meaning, signifies direction, regulation, or control. In reference to any particular state or nation, government signifies that system of fundamental rules and principles to which it is subject.

54. *Has the Christian church, in its visible form, any system of government peculiar to itself?*

Yes, the Christian church, being a spiritual kingdom, whose only King, Head, and Governor is the Lord Jesus Christ, has a system of laws enjoined by him and by which alone it is, and of right ought to be, governed; and has therefore an inherent power of self-regulation and direction.

Isaiah 9:6 — For unto us a child is born, unto us a son is given: and the government shall be upon his shoulder: and his name shall be called Wonderful, Counsellor, The mighty God, The everlasting Father, The Prince of Peace.
Colossians 1:18 — And he is the head of the body, the church: who is the beginning, the firstborn from the dead; that in all *things* he might have the preeminence.
Ephesians 1:22 — And hath put all *things* under his feet, and gave him *to be* the head over all *things* to the church...
Matthew 23:8-10 — But be not ye called Rabbi: for one is your Master, *even* Christ; and all ye are brethren. And call no *man* your father upon the earth: for one is your Father, which is in heaven. Neither be ye called masters: for one is your Master, *even* Christ.
See also John 18:36; Luke 12:14; John 6:15 and 8:15; Romans 14:17; Colossians 1:13.

55. *In what respects is the church exclusively the kingdom of Christ?*

The church is exclusively the kingdom of Christ because: it is based upon his institution; subject to his authority; regulated by his laws; animated by his Spirit; devoted to his honor; blessed by his presence; and protected by his power, as Head over all things to his church.

56. *Where, then, is that system of laws to be found by which the church is to be governed?*

In the word of God; the only infallible rule of Christian faith and practice.

Isaiah 8:20 — To the law and to the testimony: if they speak not according to this word, *it is* because *there is* no light in them.
Revelation 22:18 — For I testify unto every man that heareth the words of the prophecy of this book, If any man shall add unto these things, God shall add unto him the plagues that are written in this book...
Hebrews 8:5 — Who serve unto the example and shadow of heavenly things, as Moses was admonished of God when he was about to make the tabernacle: for, See, saith he, *that* thou make all things according to the pattern shewed to thee in the mount.

57. *Why is such a form of government necessary to the church?*

Because the Christian church is a society, and no society can exist without laws and order; and because the church, having no civil power or authority, requires a spiritual authority sufficient to preserve order, censure the disobedient, expel the rebellious, and encourage and sustain the pious.

Hebrews 13:17 — Obey them that have the rule over you, and submit yourselves: for they watch for your souls, as they that must give account, that they may do it with joy, and not with grief: for that *is* unprofitable for you.

Isaiah 33:20, 23 — Look upon Zion, the city of our solemnities: thine eyes shall see Jerusalem a quiet habitation, a tabernacle *that* shall not be taken down; not one of the stakes thereof shall ever be removed, neither shall any of the cords thereof be broken... Thy tacklings are loosed; they could not well strengthen their mast, they could not spread the sail: then is the prey of a great spoil divided; the lame take the prey.

58. *From whence is this authority of the church derived?*

The power of the church is derived from God the Father; bestowed through the Mediator, Christ Jesus; conferred by Christ; and to be exercised by those officers to whom Christ has committed the spiritual government of his church.

59. *What is meant by the divine right of church government[24]?*

By the divine right of church government, we are taught that it is not the result of human prudence, but sanctioned by divine approbation, established by divine acts, and enforced by divine precepts.

60. *In what sense do Romanists[25] and high-church[26] prelatists[27] hold this opinion?*

The Romanists and high-church prelatists hold that a particular form of church government is not only appointed by God, but is so essential to the existence of the church that there can be no true church without it.

61. *Do any Presbyterians maintain this kind of divine right, with respect to their form of church government?*

No, there are no Presbyterians guilty of this extravagance.

---

[24] Referred to in various writings of this period in Latin as *jus divinum (divine right)*. One book in particular, *Jus Divinum Reigiminus Ecclesiastici (The Divine Right of Church Government)* was written by London Ministers of the Westminster Assembly. [Ed.]

[25] Those adhering to the Roman Catholic Church. [Ed.]

[26] A reference to the Church of England; High-Church wherein are often retained images and statues and sometimes called the "English Catholic" Church because of its similarity of worship to Romanist practices. [Ed.]

[27] A reference to the bishops and higher offices found in the Roman Catholic and Episcopal systems of hierarchical church government. [Ed.]

62. *In what sense do Presbyterians hold the divine right of their system of government?*

They maintain that a particular form of church government, in its essential principles, was appointed by the authority of Christ; and that it is the duty of all churches to adopt this form; but they do not believe that the whole platform of government is laid down in detail in the word of God, nor that differences in such ecclesiastical arrangements merely, will destroy, or essentially vitiate, the character of a church.

63. *Have different forms of church government been adopted by different churches of professing Christians?*

Yes, there have been several different forms of church government adopted by different denominations of professing Christians.

Section 2
Of the Presbyterian form of church government.

64. *What form of church government do you believe to be most agreeable to the word of God, and therefore to be most properly entitled to the claim of divine right?*

That plan of church government which is denominated *Presbyterianism*.

65. *What is the origin of the word "Presbyterianism"?*

The word is taken from Scripture, in which the ministers of the church are called presbyters or elders.

Acts 14:23 — And when they had ordained them elders in every church, and had prayed with fasting, they commended them to the Lord, on whom they believed.
1 Timothy 4:14 — Neglect not the gift that is in thee, which was given thee by prophecy, with the laying on of the hands of the presbytery.

66. *Were there, in the times of the apostles, churches which were called by different names and which yet claimed to be the true churches of Christ, such as the Episcopalian church, the Roman Catholic church, etc.?*

No, we read of no such names in Scripture.

67. *By what name, then, were believers on the Lord Jesus Christ, at that time, called?*

Believers were at first called *disciples*, and afterwards *Christians*, and their churches after the place in which they were located.

68. *When were these various names, by which the church is now distinguished, introduced?*

They were introduced at various times, as different opinions arose on the subjects to which these names refer.

69.   *Why was the term "Presbyterian" applied to those by whom it is now received?*

When those scriptural principles on which the equality of ministers, and the government of the church by presbyters depend, were subverted or denied, this name was adopted to hold forth the attachment of those who embraced it, to that form of church government, and to those doctrines which are sanctioned by Scripture, in opposition to those forms and doctrines which are founded on human authority, and which had usurped their place.

70.   *Do Presbyterians acknowledge any man to be their head or founder, by whose name they are called?*

No; they call no man master on earth; neither do they acknowledge any other foundation for their system of faith and government, than the word of God.

71.   *What are the essential principles of the Presbyterian form of church government?*

The supreme Headship of Jesus Christ; the official equality of its ministers; the office of ruling elders, as representatives of the people; the election of the officers of particular churches by church members; and the authority of its several courts.

72.   *What is further essential to the constitution of the Presbyterian church?*

It is essential to the constitution of the Presbyterian church that all her pastors be equal in authority; that the government and discipline in each particular church be conducted by a bench of presbyters or elders and not by all the communicants; and that all the several churches be bound together under the authority of presbyteries and other courts[28] of review and control, as circumstances may render expedient and necessary.

73.   *Is it, then, necessary, in order to constitute any particular church Presbyterian, that it should be in formal connection with a presbytery?*

It has certainly been the unvarying doctrine of the Presbyterian church, founded on the word of God, that all particular churches should be united together, under one presbyterial government; and that any church, therefore, which remains in a state of isolated inde-

---

[28] *Presbytery* is generally considered a court in the Presbyterian church. It takes this name from the teaching of the kingship of Jesus Christ. During the time when the term "court" was adopted, most countries had kings and queens. When they deliberated matters of state with the various other counselors and officers of the state, this was referred to as the royal court. Likewise, when the elders of the kingdom of Jesus deliberated the business of the local church, they used this same term. This seems unique to Presbyterian churches of Scottish origin. Churches from Holland, Germany, Hungary, and other European countries which also used the presbyterian form of church government did not use the term "court". They use the term "court" only when the elders are handling judicial matters. *Other courts* is a reference to the synods, general and ecumenical assemblies (referred to as higher or broader courts) of the church. [Ed.]

pendency, or goes back to that condition, cannot be considered as a truly Presbyterian church.

74. *What do you mean by the supreme headship of the Lord Jesus Christ?*

By the supreme Headship of the Lord Jesus Christ, I mean, that under him the whole number of the elect shall be collected into one house and family of God; that he has given to the catholic visible church the ministry and ordinances, for the gathering and perfecting of the saints in this life, to the end of the world; that he does, by his own presence and Spirit, according to his promise, make them effectual thereunto; and that further, besides the Lord Jesus Christ, there is no other Head of the church having authority to legislate for it, or to frame laws and institute officers, binding on the consciences of men.

Psalm 2:6 — Yet have I set my king upon my holy hill of Zion.
Matthew 28:20 — Teaching them to observe all things whatsoever I have commanded you: and, lo, I am with you alway, *even* unto the end of the world. Amen.
1 Peter 5:3 — Neither as being lords over *God's* heritage, but being ensamples to the flock.
See also Matthew 27:22; Colossians 1:18; Ephesians 1:22; Matthew 23:8-10; 2 Thessalonians 2:4; Ephesians 4:11-23.

CHAPTER 3
OFFICERS OF THE CHURCH

Section 1
Of the extraordinary officers of the church
— the apostles, evangelists, and prophets.

75. *How many kinds of office-bearers did Christ appoint in his church?*

Two kinds; extraordinary and ordinary officers.

Ephesians 4:11 — And he gave some, apostles; and some, prophets; and some, evangelists; and some, pastors and teachers...

76. *What do you mean by extraordinary officers of the church?*

The extraordinary officers of the church were persons endowed with supernatural gifts and extraordinary authority; of which kind were apostles, evangelists, and prophets.

77. *For what purpose were they appointed?*

Christianity, requiring a series of miracles to attest its divine origin and inspiration to reveal all necessary truth, these officers were appointed to make known authoritatively the will of Christ; settle the constitution of the church; and commit the administration of it to ordinary and permanent officers.

Titus 1:5 — For this cause left I thee in Crete, that thou shouldest set in order the things that are wanting, and ordain elders in every city, as I had appointed thee...
2 Timothy 2:2 — And the things that thou hast heard of me among many witnesses, the same commit thou to faithful men, who shall be able to teach others also.
See also Ephesians 4:11-13.

78. *Did they have any successors in their character and duties, as extraordinary officers?*

None that we read of in the word of God; neither are we there told that any should succeed them as apostles, evangelists, or prophets.

Acts 14:23 — So when they had appointed elders in every church, and prayed with fasting, they commended them to the Lord in whom they had believed.

79. *What was necessary to constitute an apostle?*

It was necessary that the apostles should have personally seen the Lord Jesus Christ; have obtained their commission immediately from Christ; be endowed with the gift of working miracles; be able to communicate miraculous powers to others; and possess authority over all the churches in every part of the world.

1 Peter 5:1 — The elders which are among you I exhort, who am also an elder, and a witness of the sufferings of Christ, and also a partaker of the glory that shall be revealed...
1 Corinthians 9:1 — Am I not an apostle? am I not free? have I not seen Jesus Christ our Lord? are not ye my work in the Lord? *(cont'd)*

Acts 19:6 — And when Paul had laid *his* hands upon them, the Holy Ghost came on them; and they spake with tongues, and prophesied.

1 Corinthians 7:17 — But as God hath distributed to every man, as the Lord hath called every one, so let him walk. And so ordain I in all churches.

80. *Who were evangelists?*

Evangelists were extraordinary officers, suited to the infant state of the church, who were commissioned to travel under the direction and control of the apostles, that they might ordain ministers, and settle congregations, according to the system laid down by Christ and his apostles.[29]

Acts 21:8 — And the next *day* we that were of Paul's company departed, and came unto Caesarea: and we entered into the house of Philip the evangelist, which was *one* of the seven; and abode with him.

81. *Who were prophets?*

They were persons, who, under the direction and extraordinary influence of the Holy Spirit, explained the Scripture, enforced its doctrines, publicly addressed the church, and foretold events.[30]

1 Corinthians 14:1, 3, 4 — Follow after charity, and desire spiritual *gifts*, but rather that ye may prophesy... But he that prophesieth speaketh unto men *to* edification, and exhortation, and comfort... He that speaketh in an *unknown* tongue edifieth himself; but he that prophesieth edifieth the church.

82. *Were these extraordinary officers of the church exclusively occupied in the discharge of their extraordinary functions?*

No; they probably took an active part in the government of the church; while they certainly engaged in the ordinary duties of the ministry.

See Acts 10:44, 47; 15:6, 22; 21:17, 18; and 6.

---

[29] *'The work of an evangelist,"* says Eusebius, *"was this; to lay the foundation of the faith in barbarous nations; to constitute their pastors; and having committed to them the cultivating [of] those new plantations, they passed on to other countries and nations."* *"Such were evangelists,"* says Stillingfleet; *"who were sent, sometimes into this country, to put the churches in order there, sometimes into another; but, wherever they were, they acted as evangelists, **and not as fixed ministers."*** [Ed. These are not to be confused with modern day *evangelists* which is a substantially more limited use of the word *evangelist*. However, many Presbyterian Churches today do give the *power of an evangelist* to a teaching elder who may be in isolated areas (such as a missionary, so that he may be able to appoint and ordain ruling elders in the absence of a presbytery — this authority being granted only by a presbytery, when there is no local session in existence.)]

[30] See Henderson on *Inspiration*, p. 209, etc. and Lord Barrington's *Works*. vol. I. p. 33. In their ordinary character, the prophets were presbyters, as appears from Acts 13:1-3, and as is fully admitted by archbishop Potter in his work on the Church. (See pp. 101-103, etc.) So, also, in their ordinary character as ministers of Christ, the apostles expressly denominate themselves as presbyters. (See 2 & 3 John; 1 Peter 5:1; Acts 7:10; Philemon 8-9; Acts 7 :58; etc.) And by every means they identify themselves with such; while Timothy, an evangelist, was, as we are expressly taught, ordained by the hands of a presbytery. See 1 Timothy 4:14, and Potter, do. 107.

83. **In what sense, then, are the present ministers of the Gospel successors to these extraordinary officers of the apostolic churches?**

In their extraordinary character and functions, these officers can have no successors; but in their ordinary character, all ministers of the Gospel, regularly called, who maintain the doctrine of the apostles and prophets, are their true and valid successors.

1 Corinthians 12:28, 29 — And God hath set some in the church, first apostles, secondarily prophets, thirdly teachers, after that miracles, then gifts of healings, helps, governments, diversities of tongues. *Are* all apostles? *are* all prophets? *are* all teachers? *are* all workers of miracles?

1 Corinthians 13:8 — Charity never faileth: but whether *there be* prophecies, they shall fail; whether *there be* tongues, they shall cease; whether *there be* knowledge, it shall vanish away. *See also Revelation 2:2.*

Titus 1:5 — For this cause left I thee in Crete, that thou shouldest set in order the things that are wanting, and ordain elders in every city, as I had appointed thee...

Acts 2:42 — And they continued stedfastly in the apostles' doctrine and fellowship, and in breaking of bread, and in prayers.

See also Ephesians 4:11, 12; Romans 12:7, 8; 1 Timothy 3:5.

Section 2
Of the ordinary and perpetual officers of the church — and first of the presbyter[31] or bishop.[32]

84. **Who are the ordinary officers of the Christian church?**

Presbyters or elders, ruling elders[33], and deacons.

Philippians 1:1 — Paul and Timotheus, the servants of Jesus Christ, to all the saints in Christ Jesus which are at Philippi, with the bishops and deacons...

Acts 20:17 — And from Miletus he sent to Ephesus, and called the elders of the church.

85. **Is there any distinction amongst those who are called elders?**

Yes; elders are divided into the teaching elders or pastors, and the ruling elders or helps.

1 Corinthians 12:28 — And God hath set some in the church, first apostles, secondarily prophets, thirdly teachers, after that miracles, then gifts of healings, helps, governments, diversities of tongues.

86. **What warrant is there for regarding the teaching presbyter, pastor, or bishop, as an ordinary and permanent officer in the church?**

Such officers were settled by apostolic authority, in every church, as its stated ministry; they are of God's appointment; they are the fruit of Christ's exaltation; and they are called by the Holy Spirit that they may feed the church of God on earth.   *(cont'd)*

---

[31] Presbyter comes from the Greek word *presbuteros* (πρεσβυτεροσ) meaning an *old man* or *elder*. [Ed.]

[32] See Question 91 for definition. [Ed.]

[33] Note the distinction here between presbyters/bishops or elders and ruling elders. Smyth held to the Westminster Assembly position that did not count the ruling elder as a presbyter. While a ruling elder may be a participant in presbytery, he was not to be considered a presbyter, which function was reserved for the bishop or teaching elder. [Ed.]

Acts 14:23 — And when they had ordained them elders in every church, and had prayed with fasting, they commended them to the Lord, on whom they believed.

Titus 1:5 — For this cause left I thee in Crete, that thou shouldest set in order the things that are wanting, and ordain elders in every city, as I had appointed thee...

See also Ephesians 4:11, Acts 20:28.

87. *What are the duties of the pastor?*

It is the duty of the pastor to preach the Gospel, and to explain and enforce the Scriptures; to conduct the different parts of public worship; to dispense the ordinances of baptism and the Lord's supper; to administer church discipline; to oversee the religious state of persons and families; and thus to rule, in the church, according to the laws of Christ.

2 Timothy 4:3 — For the time will come when they will not endure sound doctrine; but after their own lusts shall they heap to themselves teachers, having itching ears...

Acts 13:15 — And after the reading of the law and the prophets the rulers of the synagogue sent unto them, saying, *Ye* men *and* brethren, if ye have any word of exhortation for the people, say on.

1 Corinthians 10:16 — The cup of blessing which we bless, is it not the communion of the blood of Christ? The bread which we break, is it not the communion of the body of Christ?

1 Timothy 5:20 — Them that sin rebuke before all, that others also may fear.

Acts 20:28 — Take heed therefore unto yourselves, and to all the flock, over the which the Holy Ghost hath made you overseers, to feed the church of God, which he hath purchased with his own blood.

1 Timothy 5:17 — Let the elders that rule well be counted worthy of double honour, especially they who labour in the word and doctrine.

88. *What different names has the person, who fills this office, obtained in Scripture?*

The person who fills this office has, in Scripture, obtained different names expressive of his various duties. As he has the oversight of the flock of Christ, he is termed *bishop*. As he feeds them with spiritual food, he is called *pastor*. As he serves Christ in his church, he is styled *minister*. As it is his duty to be grave and prudent, and an example to the flock, and to govern well in the house and kingdom of Christ, he is termed *presbyter*, or *elder*. As he is the messenger of God, he is denominated *the angel of the church*. As he is sent to declare the will of God to sinners, and to beseech them to be reconciled to God, through Christ, he is named *ambassador*.[34] And as he dispenses the manifold grace of God, and the ordinances instituted by Christ, he is termed *steward of the mysteries of God.*

Acts 20:28 — Take heed therefore unto yourselves, and to all the flock, over the which the Holy Ghost hath made you overseers, to feed the church of God, which he hath purchased with his own blood.

Jeremiah 3:15 — And I will give you pastors according to mine heart, which shall feed you with knowledge and understanding.

1 Peter 5:1-4 — The elders which are among you I exhort, who am also an elder, and a witness of the sufferings of Christ, and also a partaker of the glory that shall be revealed: Feed the flock of God which is among you, taking the oversight *thereof*, not by constraint, but willingly; not for filthy lucre, but of a ready mind; Neither as being lords over *God's*

---

[34] While popularly used today to refer to the role of all Christians, *ambassador* is used in Scripture solely of ministers/pastors/teaching elders. [Ed.]

heritage, but being ensamples to the flock. And when the chief Shepherd shall appear, ye shall receive a crown of glory that fadeth not away.

Revelation 2:1 — Unto the angel of the church of Ephesus write; These things saith he that holdeth the seven stars in his right hand, who walketh in the midst of the seven golden candlesticks...

2 Corinthians 5:20 — Now then we are ambassadors for Christ, as though God did beseech *you* by us: we pray *you* in Christ's stead, be ye reconciled to God.

Luke 12:42 — And the Lord said, Who then is that faithful and wise steward, whom *his* lord shall make ruler over his household, to give *them their* portion of meat in due season?

89. *Are these names expressive of different gradations of ecclesiastical authority?*

No; they are indiscriminately applied in Scripture to the same officers; so that among the ministers of the Gospel there is no other superiority to be allowed, than such as arises from the influence of age, piety, learning, or zeal.

Matthew 20:26 — But it shall not be so among you: but whosoever will be great among you, let him be your minister...

1 Timothy 5:17 — Let the elders that rule well be counted worthy of double honour, especially they who labour in the word and doctrine.

Section 3
Of the identity of bishops and presbyters.

90. *What title of the Christian pastor has been supposed to refer to a superior office in the church?*

The title of *bishop*.

91. *What is the literal meaning of the word "bishop"?*

The word *(episcopos, επίσκοποσ)* translated *bishop*, signifies an overseer.

Acts 20: 28 — Take heed therefore unto yourselves, and to all the flock, over the which the Holy Ghost hath made you overseers, to feed the church of God, which he hath purchased with his own blood.

92. *Are all presbyters called bishops in Scripture?*

Yes; they are called presbyters and bishops indiscriminately.

Acts 20:17, 28 — And from Miletus he sent to Ephesus, and called the elders of the church... Take heed therefore unto yourselves, and to all the flock, over the which the Holy Ghost hath made you overseers, to feed the church of God, which he hath purchased with his own blood.

Philippians 1:1 — Paul and Timotheus, the servants of Jesus Christ, to all the saints in Christ Jesus which are at Philippi, with the bishops and deacons... *See also Titus 1:5-7.*

1 Peter 5:1, 2 — he elders which are among you I exhort, who am also an elder, and a witness of the sufferings of Christ, and also a partaker of the glory that shall be revealed: Feed the flock of God which is among you, taking the oversight *thereof*, not by constraint, but willingly; not for filthy lucre, but of a ready mind...

See also 1 Timothy 3:1-7, 5:17-19; Acts 15:2, 4, 6, 22, 23; 1 Corinthians 12:28-30; Ephesians 4:11.

93. *Is not the pastoral office the first in the church, both for dignity and usefulness?*

Yes; teaching is more honorable, and more important, than mere ruling, which is the office ascribed to prelatic bishops;[35] and therefore a ruler, or prelate, cannot be superior to a teacher or pastor.

1 Timothy 5:17 — Let the elders that rule well be counted worthy of double honour, especially they who labour in the word and doctrine.

1 Corinthians 12:28 — And God hath set some in the church, first apostles, secondarily prophets, thirdly teachers, after that miracles, then gifts of healings, helps, governments, diversities of tongues.

94. *Is there more than one final commission, from which Christian ministers derive their office and authority?*

No; all pastors derive their office and authority from Christ by the same commission, in the same words, and for the same offices, and therefore the same official authority must belong to all.

Mark 16:15 — And he said unto them, Go ye into all the world, and preach the gospel to every creature.

95. *May it not be said, that while all bishops are presbyters, all teaching presbyters are not bishops?*

As all bishops are presbyters, so is the title of bishop, which signifies an *overseer* of the flock, applicable to all presbyters who have the oversight of some particular charge and who are therefore true Scripture bishops.[36]

96. *How may this identity of bishop and presbyter be further proved?*

Nowhere in Scripture are duties imposed on bishops, distinct from those assigned to presbyters; nor are the qualifications laid down for the one, different from those laid down for the other. On the contrary, both are to possess the same qualifications, and to discharge the same duties, and are therefore the same.

Titus 1:5, 7 — For this cause left I thee in Crete, that thou shouldest set in order the things that are wanting, and ordain elders in every city, as I had appointed thee... For a bishop must be blameless, as the steward of God; not selfwilled, not soon angry, not given to wine, no striker, not given to filthy lucre...

97. *Were Timothy and Titus prelatical bishops?*

They were not prelatical bishops; nor do they appear to have had any fixed pastoral charges. They were evangelists.[37] *(cont'd)*

---

[35] Found in hierarchical or episcopal church government (e.g. Church of England and Roman Catholic Church). [Ed.]

[36] The term, however, is also applicable to one who has filled this station, when transferred, by the authority of the church, and under its sanction, to some other field of usefulness; and, in a general sense, to all ordained ministers of the Gospel.

[37] *"Now, of this matter, (whether Timothy and Titus were indeed made bishops, the one of Ephesus, the other of Crete,) I confess I can find nothing in any writer of the first three centuries, nor any intimation that they bore that name."* Whitby (an Episcopalian), in comment pref. to Titus, *"It is*

2 Timothy 4:5-10 — But watch thou in all things, endure afflictions, do the work of an evangelist, make full proof of thy ministry. For I am now ready to be offered, and the time of my departure is at hand. I have fought a good fight, I have finished *my* course, I have kept the faith: Henceforth there is laid up for me a crown of righteousness, which the Lord, the righteous judge, shall give me at that day: and not to me only, but unto all them also that love his appearing. Do thy diligence to come shortly unto me: For Demas hath forsaken me, having loved this present world, and is departed unto Thessalonica; Crescens to Galatia, Titus unto Dalmatia.

2 Corinthians 8:23 — Whether *any do enquire* of Titus, *he is* my partner and fellowhelper concerning you: or our brethren *be enquired of, they are* the messengers of the churches, *and* the glory of Christ.

See also 2 Corinthians 12:18. See Question 54.

Section 4
Of the term angel, as used in reference to the church.

98. *What other term, in Scripture, has been supposed to refer to an office in the apostolic church, superior to the ordinary bishops or presbyters?*

The term, *angel of the church.*

99. *Where is this term used?*

It is used in reference to the seven churches of Asia, in the book of Revelation.

See Revelation 2.

100. *What is the meaning of the term "angel"?*

The word *angel* signifies a messenger, and may be applied to any servant of God that bears a message from him, which the presbyter or bishop, by the express nature of his office, does.

101. *Are these angels said to be superior to the ordinary bishops or presbyters of the churches of Asia?*

No; they are not anywhere so described.

102. *Are the bishops or presbyters of the churches of Asia named separately, so as to allow us to suppose that the angel of the church was a different officer?*

They are not.

103. *Why, then, was the term "angels" used, instead of the word bishop?*

Probably, because the whole book in which it occurs is very figurative in its style; and has, therefore, been always regarded as more difficult to be understood than any other in the whole Bible; and because a special prophetic message was communicated, through these angels, to their respective churches.[38]

---

notorious, that Timothy is nowhere called a bishop by Paul, in either of the Epistles written to him." 30, VOL. IV.

[38] It may be added, that, 1. The term *angel* is itself obscure. 2. It is used in an obscure book. 3. It is nowhere else applied in Scripture to the bishop's office, if it is here. 4. It is a term which never has been brought into use in application to this office. *'The angel and the presbyter of the*

104. *Have we reason to suppose that the term "angel" would be familiar to the apostle John, who used it, and to the Jewish, and other early Christians, to whom it was addressed?*

We have such reason in the fact that the term *angel* was the name of an officer in the Jewish synagogues, which were established in every part of the world where there were Jews.

105. *Would this use of the word "angel" by the inspired writer suggest to his readers, when first employed, the idea of an officer distinct from and superior to the ordinary bishop or presbyter of a Christian church?*

No, it would not: because, in every Jewish synagogue, there was (just as there is now in every Presbyterian church) a bishop, with a bench of elders and deacons; and this bishop was indifferently called minister, pastor, presbyter, bishop, or angel of the church; just as the bishop of a Presbyterian church might be now called bishop, presbyter, pastor, minister, or angel of the church.[39]

106. *What other meaning may be attached to the word "angel", as used in the word of God?*

It may signify the moderator, who, at that time, presided among the bishops of these several churches, and who was their official organ of communication; or it may signify these bishops, in their collective capacity. (Revelation 2:8, 10, 13)

Section 5
Of the permanence, calling, and ordination, of bishops.

107. *Is the office of pastor, or bishop, designed to be permanent in the church?*

The pastor, or bishop, being commissioned to preach the Gospel and administer its ordinances for the conversion of sinners, the edifica-

---

synagogue were congregational.' Bishop White's *Lectures on the Catechism.* Philadelphia 1813. p. 462.

[39] Dr. Lightfoot, who was himself an Episcopalian, in giving an account of the officers of the synagogue, says: *"Besides these, there was 'the public minister of the synagogue,' who prayed publicly, and took care about the reading of the law, and sometimes preached, if there were not some other to discharge this office. This person was called, 'the angel of the church,' and 'the chazan or bishop of the congregation.' The public minister of the synagogue, himself, read not the law publicly' but, every Sabbath, he called seven out of the synagogue, (on other days fewer,) whom he judged fit to read. He stood by him that read, with great care observing that he read nothing either falsely, or improperly; and calling him back, and correcting him, if he had failed in any thing. And hence he was called 'overseer.' Certainly, the signification of the word 'bishop,' and 'angel of the church,' had been determined with less noise, if recourse had been made to the proper fountains; and men had not vainly disputed about the signification of words, taken, I know not whence. The service and worship of the temple being abolished, as being ceremonial, God transplanted the worship and public adoration of God, used in the synagogues, which was moral, into the Christian church; to wit, the public ministry, public prayers, reading God's word, and preaching, etc. Hence, the names of the ministers of the Gospel were the very same, 'the angel of the church,' and 'the bishop,' which belonged to the minister in the synagogues."* See *Works,* vol. xi. p. 88.

tion of believers, and the conviction of gainsayers is, necessarily, a permanent office in the church.

Acts 26:18 — To open their eyes, *and* to turn *them* from darkness to light, and *from* the power of Satan unto God, that they may receive forgiveness of sins, and inheritance among them which are sanctified by faith that is in me.
Matthew 28:20 — Teaching them to observe all things whatsoever I have commanded you: and, lo, I am with you alway, *even* unto the end of the world. Amen.

108. *What are the qualifications of a bishop?*

To be qualified for the office of bishop, a man must give satisfactory evidence that he is sound in the faith, and that he has good talents for public speaking, sincere piety, and a blameless character.

1 Timothy 5:22 — Lay hands suddenly on no man, neither be partaker of other men's sins: keep thyself pure.
2 Timothy 2:2 — And the things that thou hast heard of me among many witnesses, the same commit thou to faithful men, who shall be able to teach others also.
Titus 2:7, 8 — In all things shewing thyself a pattern of good works: in doctrine *shewing* uncorruptness, gravity, sincerity, sound speech, that cannot be condemned; that he that is of the contrary part may be ashamed, having no evil thing to say of you.

109. *May any individual, who supposes that he possesses these qualifications, take upon himself the office of a bishop?*

No; he who properly takes upon himself the office of a bishop must be called of God.

Hebrews 5:4 — And no man taketh this honour unto himself, but he that is called of God, as *was* Aaron.
Jeremiah 23:32 — Behold, I *am* against them that prophesy false dreams, saith the LORD, and do tell them, and cause my people to err by their lies, and by their lightness; yet I sent them not, nor commanded them: therefore they shall not profit this people at all, saith the LORD.
1 Timothy 5:22 — Lay hands suddenly on no man, neither be partaker of other men's sins: keep thyself pure.
Romans 10:15 — And how shall they preach, except they be sent? as it is written, How beautiful are the feet of them that preach the gospel of peace, and bring glad tidings of good things!

110. *What do you mean by being called of God to the work of the ministry?*

This call is twofold; divine and ecclesiastical.

111. *When may an individual be said to have a divine call to the office of bishop?*

When he has given evidence that he possesses the qualifications necessary to fit him for it; and when he feels impelled by an earnest desire to enter it, that he may thereby be enabled to serve God in the Gospel of his Son.

1 Timothy 3:1 — This *is* a true saying, If a man desire the office of a bishop, he desireth a good work.
Titus 1:7-9 — For a bishop must be blameless, as the steward of God; not selfwilled, not soon angry, not given to wine, no striker, not given to filthy lucre; But a lover of hospitality, a lover of good men, sober, just, holy, temperate; Holding fast the faithful word as he hath been taught, that he may be able by sound doctrine both to exhort and to convince the gainsayers.

112. When may an individual be said to be called to the office of bishop, ecclesiastically?

When the presbytery, composed of the bishops and elders of the churches, within whose bounds he resides, receive, approve, and admit him to that office, in the hope and belief that he has been divinely called.

1 Timothy 4:14 — Neglect not the gift that is in thee, which was given thee by prophecy, with the laying on of the hands of the presbytery.
2 Timothy 2:2 — And the things that thou hast heard of me among many witnesses, the same commit thou to faithful men, who shall be able to teach others also.

113. Is there any thing, besides this call, necessary to constitute an individual a Christian bishop?

Yes; he must be ordained.

Titus 1:5 — For this cause left I thee in Crete, that thou shouldest set in order the things that are wanting, and ordain elders in every city, as I had appointed thee...
1 Timothy 2:7 — Whereunto I am ordained a preacher, and an apostle, (I speak the truth in Christ, *and* lie not;) a teacher of the Gentiles in faith and verity.

114. What is the meaning of the word "ordain"?

To *ordain* means to *appoint*; or, to *set apart* to an office; or, to *invest with a ministerial function or authority.*

115. How is the bishop, or presbyter, ordained?

He is ordained by the imposition of the hands of the ministers constituting the presbytery, and by prayer.

1 Timothy 5:22 — Lay hands suddenly on no man, neither be partaker of other men's sins: keep thyself pure.
Acts 13:3 — And when they had fasted and prayed, and laid *their* hands on them, they sent *them* away.
1 Timothy 4:14 — Neglect not the gift that is in thee, which was given thee by prophecy, with the laying on of the hands of the presbytery.

116. Is ordination necessary, in itself considered, or only as a security for the order and purity of the church?

Ordination is not to be regarded as conveying any hidden or mysterious grace or power to the person ordained. It is no more than an external and solemn form, whereby the person ordained is recognized as one who is believed to have been called, and thus authorized, by God; and who is, in this way, installed into the sacred office of the ministry. Neither is this rite to be considered so essential as that, without it, a valid ministry and a true church could not, in any possible circumstances, exist.

117. What name is applied to those who are preparing for the ministry, in the belief that they have received a divine call?

They are called *candidates* for the ministry.

118. *What name is applied to those who have been allowed by presbytery to preach, and thus prove their fitness for this work?*

They are called *licentiates*; because they have received a license, or authority, to exercise their gifts.

119. *By what other name are such persons sometimes called?*

Probationers; because, until ordained, they are on trial and may have their license withdrawn or confirmed.

120. *When an individual is ordained to the office of a bishop, is he set apart to some particular charge?*

Sometimes he is ordained by the presbytery as an evangelist,[40] or a missionary, to labor where there are no existing churches; but ordinarily he is ordained over some particular charge.

Titus 1:5 — For this cause left I thee in Crete, that thou shouldest set in order the things that are wanting, and ordain elders in every city, as I had appointed thee...
1 Peter 5:1, 2 — The elders which are among you I exhort, who am also an elder, and a witness of the sufferings of Christ, and also a partaker of the glory that shall be revealed: Feed the flock of God which is among you, taking the oversight *thereof*, not by constraint, but willingly; not for filthy lucre, but of a ready mind...
Acts 20:17, 28 — And from Miletus he sent to Ephesus, and called the elders of the church... Take heed therefore unto yourselves, and to all the flock, over the which the Holy Ghost hath made you overseers, to feed the church of God, which he hath purchased with his own blood.

Section 6
Of ruling elders

121. *What is the next officer in the church, after the bishop, or presbyter?*

The ruling elder.[41]

122. *Why is this officer called the ruling elder?*

Because he is appointed to assist the bishop, who is the teaching elder, in the government of the church; and from whom he is, in this way, distinguished, by being called the ruling elder.

123. *Whence was this name derived?*

From the order of the Jewish synagogue, in which, besides a bishop, who was also called presbyter or elder, there was a bench of elders, who were associated with the bishop in authority.

124. *What powers did these elders possess in the Jewish synagogue?*

The general powers of government and discipline.

---

[40] This term is used here in a sense different, though also similar, to the term *evangelist* as it is defined in the New Testament. See Question 80 and footnotes. [Ed.]

[41] See footnote to Question 127 for further insight into Dr. Smyth's use of the term *ruling elder* — a term he considered confusing to the Presbyterian Church. [Ed.]

125. *Are ruling elders recognized in Scripture?*

They are; for we read there of helps and governments, and of the brethren who were associated with the apostles and presbyters in the early councils of the church.

1 Corinthians 12:28 — And God hath set some in the church, first apostles, secondarily prophets, thirdly teachers, after that miracles, then gifts of healings, helps, governments, diversities of tongues.
See also Romans 12:18; Acts 2:15, 26; 6:1-6 and 15; Matthew 18:15-17.

126. *From what other consideration may we deduce the necessity and scriptural propriety of ruling elders?*

The power of the church was vested by Christ in the whole body of its members; but as these cannot all meet together to transact business, or all act as officers, there must be ruling elders or delegates appointed by them for these purposes.

127. *What passage of Scripture is most generally regarded as expressly alluding to ruling elders?*

That passage in which the apostle Paul says, "let the elders that rule well be counted worthy of double honor, especially they who labor in word and doctrine." 1 Timothy 5:17[42]

128. *What is the general duty of ruling elders?*

To act with the bishop or pastor, as *helps and governments* in the exercise of ecclesiastical authority; and to watch over the flock, assist in the admission or exclusion of members, warn and censure the unruly, visit and comfort the afflicted, instruct the young, and exhort and pray as opportunity may be given.

129. *Do ruling elders possess authority equally with the bishops, as rulers of the church?*

Yes, as rulers, though not as teachers.[43]

---

[42] Dr. Smyth puts this question and answer in his catechism to show where the term *ruling elder* came from. He disagreed that this text was the Biblical authority for the office of ruling elder and claimed that the Westminster Assembly held likewise. He believed it was for this reason that the Form of Church-Government (see *Westminster Confession of Faith*, p. 402, Other Church Governors, Free Presbyterian Publications) said of church governors, "which officers reformed churches commonly call Elders." While not agreeing with this confusing terminology applied to the church governor, it was in such common usage, that he believed the Assembly acquiesced to it enough to note the common usage. Consequently, he contended that this confusing distinction of teaching elder and ruling elder remained to his day. Yet it was Smyth's considered opinion and that of the Westminster Divines as an Assembly (in his and other's opinions), that the church-governor was a completely different office than that of teaching elder. Smyth uses the term *ruling elder* hereafter, only because it would have been disconcerting for the average person to hear the proper Westminster Assembly term *church governor*. For a thorough treatment of this subject, see Smyth's *Theories of the Eldership*, Dr. Peter Campbell's *The Theory of Ruling Eldership* and the London Minister's *The Divine Right of Church Government*, Chap. 10, pp. 97-191. All available from Reformation Media and Press. [Ed.]

[43] It may be objected by some, on the basis of **1 Timothy 3:3**, that a ruling elder should be as "apt to teach" as a teaching elder. Smyth's position, and that of the Westminster Assembly, was that 1 Timothy 3 did not give requirements for governors/rulers/ruling elders, but for bishops/pastors/

130. *In what respect are they, with other members of the church, to be in subjection to the bishop?*

As the bishop is ordained not only to rule, but also to teach, elders are equally bound, with the other members of the church, to obey him in the Lord, and to receive his instructions, as far as they are agreeable to the word of God.

1 Timothy 5:17 — Let the elders that rule well be counted worthy of double honour, especially they who labour in the word and doctrine.
1 Peter 5:1 — The elders which are among you I exhort, who am also an elder, and a witness of the sufferings of Christ, and also a partaker of the glory that shall be revealed...
Hebrews 13:17 — Obey them that have the rule over you, and submit yourselves: for they watch for your souls, as they that must give account, that they may do it with joy, and not with grief: for that *is* unprofitable for you.

131. *Is it necessary that such officers should be associated with the pastor, for the wise management of the affairs of the congregation?*

As the bishop or pastor of a congregation must employ a good part of his time in studying the Scriptures; in preparing for preaching; in qualifying himself by various reading, for the defense of the Gospel; in attending upon the judicatories [courts] of the church; in watching over the general concerns of the church, and in promoting its welfare; the cooperation of such officers is altogether indispensable to the prosperity of any congregation.

Acts 6:2-4 — Then the twelve called the multitude of the disciples *unto them*, and said, It is not reason that we should leave the word of God, and serve tables. Wherefore, brethren, look ye out among you seven men of honest report, full of the Holy Ghost and wisdom, whom we may appoint over this business. But we will give ourselves continually to prayer, and to the ministry of the word.
See also James 5:14; Acts 15:4-6.

132. *What are the qualifications necessary for the office of ruling elder?*

The qualifications for the office of ruling elder are, sincere piety, sound principles, a capacity for judging, prudence, zeal, and unblemished reputation.

2 Timothy 2:21 — If a man therefore purge himself from these, he shall be a vessel unto honour, sanctified, and meet for the master's use, *and* prepared unto every good work.
1 Chronicles 12:32 — And of the children of Issachar, *which were men* that had understanding of the times, to know what Israel ought to do; the heads of them *were* two hundred; and all their brethren *were* at their commandment.
1 Timothy 3:4-7 — One that ruleth well his own house, having his children in subjection with all gravity; (For if a man know not how to rule his own house, how shall he take care of the church of God?) Not a novice, lest being lifted up with pride he fall into the condemnation of the devil. Moreover he must have a good report of them which are without; lest he fall into reproach and the snare of the devil.

---

teaching elders. They held that qualifications for rulers had been given in the Old Testament (Deuteronomy 1 reviewing Exodus 18) and did not need to be introduced anew in the New Testament. They believed that rulers were not required to be able to teach and, in fact, were not to be considered teachers in the same sense that pastors were. [Ed.]

133.   *Whom do ruling elders represent in the church?*

As the pastor represents the ministry, so ruling elders represent the members of the church.

134.   *By whom are ruling elders chosen to their office?*

As they represent the members of the church, so are they elected to their office by them.

135.   *How are ruling elders invested with their office?*

Having been called by the church, and elected by it, they are solemnly set apart to their office with prayer, or with prayer and the imposition of hands.

136.   *What number of elders should there be in every church?*

Such a number as will enable them fully to discharge all the duties incumbent upon them, towards all its members.

Section 7
Of deacons

137.   *What is the third spiritual officer in the church?*

The deacon.

138.   *Is it part of the duty of the deacon to teach, or to rule in the church?*

No; it is not said to be the duty of deacons either to teach or to rule, in any part of Scripture.

139.   *How is the office of deacon distinguished from that of ruling elder?*

The ruling elder, as a representative of the people[44], sits as a spiritual officer in all the judicatories of the church; but deacons are officers only of that particular church by whose members they are elected and are not competent, therefore, to sit as members in any one of the judicatories of the church.

140.   *What is declared in Scripture to be the express duty for which deacons were appointed?*

Deacons were appointed for the purpose of managing the temporal affairs of the church and especially to attend to the needs of the poor, by inspecting their situation and supplying their wants.

Acts 6:1-3 — And in those days, when the number of the disciples was multiplied, there arose a murmuring of the Grecians against the Hebrews, because their widows were neglected in the daily ministration. Then the twelve called the multitude of the disciples *unto them*, and said, It is not reason that we should leave the word of God, and serve tables. Wherefore, brethren, look ye out among you seven men of honest report, full of the Holy Ghost and wisdom, whom we may appoint over this business.   *(cont'd)*

---

[44] The ruling elder always sits on the session or consistory, but sits on the presbytery or other judicatories only when delegated this responsibility by his church. [Ed.]

1 Timothy 3:8 — Likewise *must* the deacons *be* grave, not doubletongued, not given to much wine, not greedy of filthy lucre…

141. *But did not Philip, who was appointed a deacon, afterwards teach and baptize?*

Not while he was a deacon, so far as can be known from any record in the word of God; but when afterwards he became an evangelist, he then received and exercised authority to teach and baptize.

Acts 21:8 — And the next *day* we that were of Paul's company departed, and came unto Caesarea: and we entered into the house of Philip the evangelist, which was *one* of the seven; and abode with him.

142. *Is there a necessity for such officers as deacons in the church of Christ?*

Christian congregations should make provision for those among them who are incapable of procuring for themselves the necessaries of life; and officers are very requisite to find out and visit such persons, and to manage the funds raised for their support.

143. *Is it very advisable that the temporal relief given by the church should be administered separately from its spiritual instructions and consolations?*

This is very advisable to prevent hypocrisy and an undervaluing of such spiritual communications.

144. *What are the qualifications necessary for a deacon?*

A deacon should posses piety, integrity, diligence, and respectability.

1 Timothy 3:8-12 — Likewise *must* the deacons *be* grave, not doubletongued, not given to much wine, not greedy of filthy lucre; 9 Holding the mystery of the faith in a pure conscience. And let these also first be proved; then let them use the office of a deacon, being *found* blameless. Even so *must their* wives *be* grave, not slanderers, sober, faithful in all things. Let the deacons be the husbands of one wife, ruling their children and their own houses well.

145. *In the distribution of the funds to the poor, are the deacons responsible, and in subordination, to the teaching and ruling elders?*

They are; for we find that, even after their appointment, the apostles and elders had in trust the collections made for the poor.

Acts 11:30 — Which also they did, and sent it to the elders by the hands of Barnabas and Saul.

146. *How are deacons elected to their office?*

They are elected by the suffrages of the members of the churches to which they belong; and are set apart by prayer and the imposition of the hands of the pastor and elders.

See Acts 6.

Section 8
Of the election of officers.

147. *Have the members of churches an undoubted right to choose their own pastor, elders, and deacons?*

Yes; churches, in common with all other free societies, have this privilege.

Acts 1:15, 26 — And in those days Peter stood up in the midst of the disciples, and said, (the number of names together were about an hundred and twenty,)… And they gave forth their lots; and the lot fell upon Matthias; and he was numbered with the eleven apostles.
Acts 6:5 — And the saying pleased the whole multitude: and they chose Stephen, a man full of faith and of the Holy Ghost, and Philip, and Prochorus, and Nicanor, and Timon, and Parmenas, and Nicolas a proselyte of Antioch…
2 Corinthians 8:19 — And not *that* only, but who was also chosen of the churches to travel with us with this grace, which is administered by us to the glory of the same Lord, and *declaration of* your ready mind:

148. *How should church members discharge this duty?*

In a spirit of meekness, humility, peace, and prayer; with a supreme regard to the glory of Christ and the spiritual interests of the church; and without partiality or respect of persons.

Philippians 2:3 — *Let* nothing *be done* through strife or vainglory; but in lowliness of mind let each esteem other better than themselves.
Acts 1:24 — And they prayed, and said, Thou, Lord, which knowest the hearts of all *men*, shew whether of these two thou hast chosen,
1 Corinthians 10:31 — Whether therefore ye eat, or drink, or whatsoever ye do, do all to the glory of God.
James 3:17 — But the wisdom that is from above is first pure, then peaceable, gentle, *and* easy to be intreated, full of mercy and good fruits, without partiality, and without hypocrisy.

CHAPTER 4
COURTS OF THE CHURCH

Section 1
Of ecclesiastical courts in general.

149.   What is meant by an ecclesiastical court?

An ecclesiastical court is an assembly of those who have the original and inherent power or authority of executing laws and distributing justice according to the constitution; *and, in general, to order whatever pertains to the spiritual welfare of the churches under their care.*[45]

150.   Is it lawful, for the exercise of ecclesiastical authority, that the rulers of the Christian church should meet in regularly organized courts?[46]

It is both lawful and necessary.

Acts 15:6 — And the apostles and elders came together for to consider of this matter. **Matthew 18:15-20** — Moreover if thy brother shall trespass against thee, go and tell him his fault between thee and him alone: if he shall hear thee, thou hast gained thy brother. But if he will not hear *thee, then* take with thee one or two more, that in the mouth of two or three witnesses every word may be established. And if he shall neglect to hear them, tell *it* unto the church: but if he neglect to hear the church, let him be unto thee as an heathen man and a publican. Verily I say unto you, Whatsoever ye shall bind on earth shall be bound in heaven: and whatsoever ye shall loose on earth shall be loosed in heaven. Again I say unto you, That if two of you shall agree on earth as touching any thing that they shall ask, it shall be done for them of my Father which is in heaven. For where two or three are gathered together in my name, there am I in the midst of them.
1 Corinthians 14:33 — For God is not *the author* of confusion, but of peace, as in all churches of the saints.

151.   How many kinds of church courts are there?

Four; the session, presbytery, synod, and general assembly.[47]

152.   Of whom are these several courts composed?

Of bishops and ruling elders, as representatives of the ministers[48] and the people.[49]

---

[45] See *Confession of Faith*, 31:2; and *Form of Government*, ch. 9-12 [this latter reference being in the Presbyterian Church in the United States' *Form of Government*. Ed.]

[46] see footnote to Q. 72 on "courts"

[47] In smaller Presbyterian denominations, not all these levels necessarily exist.

[48] bishops

[49] ruling elders

Section 2
Of the church session.

153. *What is the church session?*

The church session is composed of the pastor, when there is one, and the ruling elders, of any particular congregation, met together as a church court.

154. *What scriptural authority is there for the church sessions, or, as they may be termed, congregational presbyteries?*

Scripture teaches us, that there was a plurality of elders in the churches formed by the apostles; to whom was committed the government of the church, and who, in order to act together, must of necessity have met in council.

Acts 14:23 — And when they had ordained them elders in every church, and had prayed with fasting, they commended them to the Lord, on whom they believed.
Titus 1:5 — For this cause left I thee in Crete, that thou shouldest set in order the things that are wanting, and ordain elders in every city, as I had appointed thee...
See also Matthew 18:15-20.

155. *What further evidence does Scripture afford, for such church courts?*

The titles, given by the Holy Spirit to ecclesiastical offices and officers, are such as impart a power of judging causes; and express the same authority which the elders in Israel were accustomed to exercise in ecclesiastical matters.

156. *What are some of these titles?*

The officers of the church are called guides, or leaders[50], bishops, or overseers[51], elders[52], rulers[53], heads[54], and governors.

157. *How should the business of the session be conducted?*

The meeting of the session should be constituted by prayer, each member being called upon by the moderator (who is, by right of office, the pastor or minister present) to give his opinion, and every question being decided by a majority of votes.

158. *Who are subject to the authority of the session?*

All the members of that particular church, in which the session exists.

---

[50] Hebrews 13:7, 17, 24, comp. with Joshua 13:21; Deuteronomy 1:13; Micah 3:9; Acts 7:10, 23, 24, 26, 33; 1 Peter 2:14
[51] Acts 20: 28 ff. comp. with Numbers 31:14; Judges 9:28; 2 Kings 11:15, in the Greek
[52] Acts 14:23 ff., comp. with Judges 8:14; Ruth 4:2, 3; 2 Samuel 5:3; 1 Chronicles 11:3
[53] Acts 23:5, with Exodus 22:28. Matthew 9:18; Luke 8:41; John 3:1; Romans 12:8; 1 Thessalonians 5:12; 1 Timothy 5:17
[54] Deuteronomy 1:13; Micah 3:9

159. *Over what matters has the church session authority?*

The church session is charged with maintaining the spiritual government of the congregation; for which purpose they have power to inquire into the knowledge and Christian conduct of the members of the church; to admonish, to rebuke, to suspend or exclude from the sacraments those who are found to deserve censure; to concert [decide/coordinate] the best measures for promoting the spiritual interests of the congregation; and to appoint delegates to the higher judicatories of the church.

Hebrews 13:17 — Obey them that have the rule over you, and submit yourselves: for they watch for your souls, as they that must give account, that they may do it with joy, and not with grief: for that *is* unprofitable for you.
See also 1 Thessalonians 5:12, 13; 1 Timothy 5:17; Ezekiel 34:4; 2 Thessalonians 6:6, 14, 15; 1 Corinthians 12:27; Acts 15:2, 6.

160. *How are matters to be brought up before the session for its judgment upon them?*

Either by an elder, or by any member of the church presenting a memorial,[55] or bringing[56] a complaint, or making[57] charges.

161. *Is there any appeal from the judgment of the session, by a party supposing himself aggrieved?*

Yes; there is an appeal from the session to the presbytery.

162. *What is the duty of the members of the church, towards their session?*

To respect and uphold their authority, as given to them by Christ; to render a cheerful obedience to their decisions, as in the Lord; cordially to cooperate with them, in those plans of usefulness they recommend; to strengthen their hands by prayer; to honor their character, though, like themselves, imperfect men; and to receive and seek their advice in all spiritual difficulties and distresses.

1 Thessalonians 5:12, 13 — And we beseech you, brethren, to know them which labour among you, and are over you in the Lord, and admonish you; And to esteem them very highly in love for their work's sake. *And* be at peace among yourselves.
See also Hebrews 13:17.

Section 3
Of the presbytery.

163. *What is the next court of the church?*

The presbytery.

164. *What is the meaning of the term "presbytery"?*

It simply means an assembly of elders.

---

[55] A eulogy or other praise of someone's good character placed in the minutes as a memorial to him or her. [Ed.]

[56] Original, *preferring* [Ed.].

[57] Original, *tabling* [Ed.].

165. *How is the presbytery, considered as a court of the church, constituted?*

A presbytery consists of all the ministers, and one ruling elder from each congregation, within a certain district.

166. *What is the extent of its jurisdiction?*

The authority of the presbytery extends to its own members, and to the several sessions and congregations belonging to it.

167. *What is the design and use of a presbytery?*

It is a court of appeal from church sessions; it affords an opportunity for mutual consultation and advice; it is a bond of visible union; an authority, to which common submission is due, and by which is ordered whatever pertains to the spiritual welfare of the churches under its care.

168. *What is the Scriptural warrant for presbyteries, as courts of the church?*

The first argument is found in the ordinance of God, instituted by Moses, by which particular congregations were taught to bring their hard and difficult controversies to a superior ecclesiastical judicatory. This order was reestablished by Jehoshaphat, who established an ecclesiastical senate at Jerusalem, to receive complaints and judge[58] causes brought before them. This form of government is also commended unto us by David, as the praise of Jerusalem. So that the ecclesiastical assemblies and synagogues in Israel were not independent, but were under the government of superior courts.

See Deuteronomy 17:8-12; 2 Chronicles 19:8-11; Psalm 122:4, 5.

169. *But how does this establish[59] any authority for such courts now?*

Because they formed no part of the ceremonial law, but were based upon the principles of common and perpetual equity[60]; and therefore are such courts equally in accord with the Divine will, and advantageous to the church now.

170. *What other argument can you give for the establishment of such courts in the Christian church?*

They are required by that rule of discipline laid down by our Lord, for its government: *tell it unto the church.* For, since Christ here gave no new rule, the Christian church not being organized, but appeals to one already familiar, he must have referred to the practice of the synagogue discipline already described; and must, therefore,

---

[58] Original, *adjudge* [Ed.]

[59] Original, *afford* [Ed.].

[60] Consult Westminster Confession of Faith 19:4 and Larger Catechism 120 [Ed.].

be considered as teaching that particular churches are not independent, but are to be in subjection to superior judicatories.[61]

See Matthew 18:15-20.

171. How is this supported biblically?

Our Saviour here points out to us, in cases of offense among brethren, three degrees of admonition; a censure to be passed upon contempt of this admonition; and, finally, excommunication, in case of obstinate impenitence. But we know that this is exactly in accord with the Jewish plan, and that this very authority among them was committed to their councils.[62]

See Leviticus 19:18; Proverbs 11:13; Deuteronomy 17:9-11; 19:15; 2 Chronicles 19:10; Exodus 12:19; Numbers 15:30, 31, and Galatians 5:12; Ezra 10:8; and Galatians 1:9. Matthew 9:11; Luke 15:2; Acts 11:2; 21:28, 29. See also Calvin and Beza on Matthew 18:17.

172. May we not also establish the authority of such courts by a reference to the practice of the apostles and the order of the first churches?

Yes; the Scriptures prove that several distinct congregations were regarded as one church, and were under one common government.

1 Timothy 4:14 — Neglect not the gift that is in thee, which was given thee by prophecy, with the laying on of the hands of the presbytery.

Acts 15:2, 4, 6 — When therefore Paul and Barnabas had no small dissension and disputation with them, they determined that Paul and Barnabas, and certain other of them, should go up to Jerusalem unto the apostles and elders about this question... And when they were come to Jerusalem, they were received of the church, and *of* the apostles and elders, and they declared all things that God had done with them... And the apostles and elders came together for to consider of this matter.

173. What illustration can you give?

The several cases of the churches in Jerusalem, Antioch, Ephesus, Corinth, and Samaria.

Section 4
Of a presbytery at Jerusalem.

174. How may it be inferred that there were more congregations than one at Jerusalem?

First, from the great number of converts that were added to that church.[63]

Acts 2:41, 42, 46 — Then they that gladly received his word were baptized: and the same day there were added unto them about three thousand souls... And they continued stedfastly in the apostles' doctrine and fellowship, and in breaking of bread, and in prayers...

---

[61] Primarily and particularly in matters pertaining to doctrine and discipline. It is generally considered among biblical Presbyterians that *pious advice* can be given in other areas, but submission is required only in matters of doctrine and discipline and then only when consistent with Scripture. [Ed.]

[62] See also Paget, on the *Power of Classes and Synods*, London, 1641, p. 35, etc.

[63] There were no places large enough for such meetings, so they met in houses. [Ed.]

And they, continuing daily with one accord in the temple, and breaking bread from house to house, did eat their meat with gladness and singleness of heart...

Acts 4:4 — Howbeit many of them which heard the word believed; and the number of the men was about five thousand.

Acts 5:14 — And believers were the more added to the Lord, multitudes both of men and women.

Acts 6:1 — And in those days, when the number of the disciples was multiplied, there arose a murmuring of the Grecians against the Hebrews, because their widows were neglected in the daily ministration.

Acts 21:20 — And when they heard it, they glorified the Lord, and said unto him, Thou seest, brother, how many thousands of Jews there are which believe; and they are all zealous of the law...

Acts 9:31 — Then had the churches rest throughout all Judaea and Galilee and Samaria, and were edified; and walking in the fear of the Lord, and in the comfort of the Holy Ghost, were multiplied.

Acts 12:24 — But the word of God grew and multiplied. *Compare Acts 1:15.*

Secondly, from the many apostles and other preachers who labored in that church.

See the preceding references.

Thirdly, from the diversity of language found among these believers, and thus requiring the necessity for distinct assemblies.

See Acts 2 and 6.

Fourthly, from the fact that the Lord's supper was administered in different houses at the same time.

Acts 2:46 — And they, continuing daily with one accord in the temple, and breaking bread from house to house, did eat their meat with gladness and singleness of heart...

175. *How may it be shown, that these several congregations were under one presbyterial government?*

First, because all these congregations are denominated one church.

Acts 8:1 — And Saul was consenting unto his death. And at that time there was a great persecution against the church which was at Jerusalem; and they were all scattered abroad throughout the regions of Judaea and Samaria, except the apostles.

Acts 2:47 — Praising God, and having favour with all the people. And the Lord added to the church daily such as should be saved.

Acts 5:11 — And great fear came upon all the church, and upon as many as heard these things.

See also Acts 12 and Acts 15:4.

Secondly, because the elders of the church are expressly mentioned.

Acts 11:30 — Which also they did, and sent it to the elders by the hands of Barnabas and Saul.

Acts 15:4, 6, 22 — And when they were come to Jerusalem, they were received of the church, and *of* the apostles and elders, and they declared all things that God had done with them... And the apostles and elders came together for to consider of this matter... Then pleased it the apostles and elders, with the whole church, to send chosen men of their own company to Antioch with Paul and Barnabas; *namely,* Judas surnamed Barsabas, and Silas, chief men among the brethren...

Acts 21:17, 18 — And when we were come to Jerusalem, the brethren received us gladly. And the *day* following Paul went in with us unto James; and all the elders were present.

Thirdly, because the apostles performed the duty of presbyters, in the church of Jerusalem.

Acts 10:44, 47 — While Peter yet spake these words, the Holy Ghost fell on all them which heard the word… Can any man forbid water, that these should not be baptized, which have received the Holy Ghost as well as we?

Acts 21:17, 18 — And when we were come to Jerusalem, the brethren received us gladly. And the *day* following Paul went in with us unto James; and all the elders were present. *See also Acts 6 and Acts 15:6, 22.*

Fourthly, because these presbyters and elders met together, as one body, for acts of government.

See as before and Acts 15:6, 22; 21:17, 18.

Fifthly, because, while they worshipped God and observed his ordinances in different assemblies, they were, nevertheless, united under one common government.

Acts 2:16 — But this is that which was spoken by the prophet Joel…

Acts 2:44 — And all that believed were together, and had all things common…

176. ***But granting there were many different congregations at Jerusalem, united under one presbytery, are we to consider this example binding upon other churches?***

It was expressly foretold that out of Zion should come forth the law, and the word of the Lord from Jerusalem; and since the apostles continued together for some years at Jerusalem, we must necessarily conclude, that the government of this church was left for our imitation, and that in the constitution of all other churches, their members were united together like it, under the direction of presbyteries.[64]

Isaiah 2. Philippians 3.

Section 5
Of a presbytery at Ephesus, and in other places.

177. ***May the same conclusion be inferred respecting the church at Ephesus?***

Yes; first, from the length of time the apostles labored there.

Acts 20:31 — Therefore watch, and remember, that by the space of three years I ceased not to warn every one night and day with tears.

Secondly, from the success which attended their preaching.

Acts 19:20 — So mightily grew the word of God and prevailed.

Acts 17:18 — Then certain philosophers of the Epicureans, and of the Stoicks, encountered him. And some said, What will this babbler say? other some, he seemeth to be a setter forth of strange gods: because he preached unto them Jesus, and the resurrection.

Thirdly, from the number of believers found there.

Acts 19:17-20 — And this was known to all the Jews and Greeks also dwelling at Ephesus; and fear fell on them all, and the name of the Lord Jesus was magnified. And many that believed came, and confessed, and shewed their deeds. Many of them also which used

---

[64] See Bastwick's *Utter Routing*, pp. 463ff.

curious arts brought their books together, and burned them before all *men*: and they counted the price of them, and found *it* fifty thousand *pieces* of silver. So mightily grew the word of God and prevailed.

Fourthly, from the reasons Paul assigned for his continuance there.

1 Corinthians 16:8, 9 — But I will tarry at Ephesus until Pentecost. For a great door and effectual is opened unto me, and *there are* many adversaries.

Fifthly, from the multitude of bishops or pastors there.

Acts 20:17, 28 — And from Miletus he sent to Ephesus, and called the elders of the church... Take heed therefore unto yourselves, and to all the flock, over the which the Holy Ghost hath made you overseers, to feed the church of God, which he hath purchased with his own blood.

Sixthly, from the mention of one of these congregations, in such a way as to imply the existence of others.

1 Corinthians 16:19 — The churches of Asia salute you. Aquila and Priscilla salute you much in the Lord, with the church that is in their house.
Revelation 2:17 — [To THE CHURCH of Ephesus. Ed.] He that hath an ear, let him hear what the Spirit saith unto the churches; To him that overcometh will I give to eat of the hidden manna, and will give him a white stone, and in the stone a new name written, which no man knoweth saving he that receiveth *it*.

Seventhly, from the evident union of these churches under one presbyterial government.[65]

Revelation 2:1, 2, 6, 17 — Unto the angel of THE CHURCH of Ephesus write... He that hath an ear, let him hear what the Spirit saith unto THE CHURCHES...[66]

178. *May the same inferences be made as to the churches at Corinth, and at Antioch, at Caesarea, and at Samaria?*

Yes; as appears from there being more churches than one in these cities; while they are, nevertheless, called one church; and also from there being many pastors there at the same time.

See as to Corinth, Acts 13:1, and 18:7-10; 1 Corinthians 1:2; 14:20; 13:34; 14:3, 4; 5:4, 5; 2 Corinthians 2:6. As to Antioch, Acts 11:19, 20, 25, 29, 30; 13:1, 5; 15:35. As to Samaria, Acts 8:5 ,6, 12, 14. As to Caesarea, Acts 11:30.

Section 6
Of the presbytery — concluded.

179. *You have now established the authority of presbyteries from the discipline of the synagogue, from our Saviour's positive rule, and from the order of the apostolic churches. Is there any other source of evidence?*

Yes; in the practice of the apostles, as we shall see when we consider the case of the synodical assembly at Jerusalem.

Acts 15.

---

[65] An eighth argument, is this: The church of Ephesus consisted of both Jews and Gentiles, as appears from **Acts 18**. Paul desired to stay with the Jews, to whom, as appears from chapter 19:8, he preached for three months; and yet the Epistle of the Ephesians is addressed especially to those who were heathen, when there must have been one or more congregations of converted Jews.

[66] The point here is that the church in Ephesus (singular) is later referred to as composed of churches (plural) in v. 17 [Ed.]

180. *Is it necessary that all churches should be thus united together in one presbyterial government?*[67]

All the churches of Christ are certainly under obligation to conform to that primitive and scriptural order which is divinely authorized.

Philippians 4:9 — Those things, which ye have both learned, and received, and heard, and seen in me, do: and the God of peace shall be with you.

181. *Why are they under this obligation?*

Because the church, being a divine institution and not a mere voluntary or human society, particular churches are not at liberty to set aside any of the rules of Christ's kingdom, and are therefore bound, if they have opportunity, to combine themselves into presbyteries for their spiritual government.

182. *Do they, by neglecting this order, commit evil?*

Yes; all that neglect it offend against the communion of saints, and walk not as members of the Body of Christ.

See Romans 12:5. 1 Corinthians 12:25. Ephesians 4:16.

183. *Do congregations, and their members, owe submission to the decrees of their presbyteries?*

Such decrees are recognized by Jesus Christ, so far as they are in accord with his statutes, as contained in the word of God; and to resist them, therefore, is, in such a case, to despise the authority of Christ.

Matthew 16:19 —And I will give unto thee the keys of the kingdom of heaven: and whatsoever thou shalt bind on earth shall be bound in heaven: and whatsoever thou shalt loose on earth shall be loosed in heaven.
Isaiah 8:20 — To the law and to the testimony: if they speak not according to this word, *it is* because *there is* no light in them.
See also Acts 4:19.

184. *Of what sin are churches guilty, who thus reject the scriptural determinations of their ecclesiastical courts?*[68]

Those churches which reject the sentence and determination of their church courts, when consonant to Scripture, commit a double sin; first, by transgressing against the written word of God; and secondly, by despising the ordinance of God, and throwing contempt upon the authority of his officers. For churches are just as much bound to their superior courts as are individual members to their particular churches; that is, so far as they act according to the truth and will of God.

---

[67] See this fully advanced by Alexander Henderson, as quoted in Dr. McCrie's *Miscell. Writ.* p.86.

[68] Note here that there is no suggestion that matters of advice, preference or convenience are mentioned. Thus, sin is involved when there is rejection of court and doctrinal judgments. [Ed.]

185. *Is there any appeal from the decision of the presbytery?*

Yes; an appeal can be taken from the decision of the presbytery to the synod.

Section 7
Of the synod.[69]

186. *What is the third court of the church?*

The synod.

187. *What is the meaning of the term "synod".*

The word *synod* means an assembly of persons, of one faith, and for the same purpose.

188. *Why, then, is this church court called a synod?*

As the presbytery is a convention of the bishops and elders within a certain district, so a synod is a convention of the bishops and elders within a district so large as to include within it at least three presbyteries; or it may be defined as a larger presbytery.

189. *What is the scriptural warrant for holding synodical assemblies?*

A synod composed of the rulers from several churches met, disputed, and determined a subject then controverted in the churches, in the city of Jerusalem; as is recorded in the Acts of the Apostles.

See Acts 15; Ephesians 4:11-16.

190. *Is there any other ground on which the authority for holding such assemblies rests?*

Yes; they are in accordance with the procedure of the Jewish synagogues, which were all subordinate to the Sanhedrin, or ecclesiastical court, held in Jerusalem, to which Christ refers with approval;[70] and which were the model after which the Christian church was fashioned.

See Matthew chap. 18, compared with Deuteronomy 17:8-12. See also Matthew 13:54; Mark 6:2; Luke 4:6, and 7:5; James 2:2; Revelation 2:9.

191. *Does the power [authority] of the synod interfere with that of the presbytery?*

No; it is designed to strengthen that power [authority], and extend it.

---

[69] In many denominations, there may only be presbyteries and general assemblies. Synods may be omitted as in the case of the Orthodox Presbyterian Church, the Presbyterian Church in America and many other denominations that are smaller. In some cases, general assemblies are called general synods, though this practice is more common among the continental/reformed denominations than among Presbyterians. [Ed.]

[70] Original, *approbation* [Ed.].

192. *What power does the synod possess?*

The synod has power to receive and issue all appeals, and to decide on all references brought up from presbyteries; to review their proceedings; and generally to take such order with respect to presbyteries, sessions, and people under their care, as may be in conformity with the word of God and for the advancement of the kingdom of Christ.

193. *Is there any appeal from the judgment of the synod?*

Yes; there is an appeal to the general assembly, the greatest and highest court of the church.

Section 8
Of the general assembly.

194. *How, then, do you describe the general assembly?*

It is the highest judicatory of the church representing, in one body or court, through their bishops and elders, which are delegated by the presbyteries, all the particular congregations under its jurisdiction; it being, in fact, a larger synod.

195. *Is there any warrant for such an assembly of the rulers of the church, in the Scriptures?*

There is warrant for it in the council held at Jerusalem, as recorded in the fifteenth chapter of Acts.

1 Corinthians 14:40 — Let all things be done decently and in order.
Ezekiel 43:12 — This *is* the law of the house; Upon the top of the mountain the whole limit thereof round about *shall be* most holy. Behold, this *is* the law of the house.
See also 2 Chronicles 19:8.

196. *Will you state the grounds of this opinion?*

First, a question which arose at Antioch, affecting the faith and practice of all the churches of Christ, was referred for settlement to this assembly.

Acts 15:2 — When therefore Paul and Barnabas had no small dissension and disputation with them, they determined that Paul and Barnabas, and certain other of them, should go up to Jerusalem unto the apostles and elders about this question.

Secondly, this assembly consisted of the rulers of the church, while it was open to the people.

Acts 15:6, 12 — And the apostles and elders came together for to consider of this matter... Then all the multitude kept silence, and gave audience to Barnabas and Paul, declaring what miracles and wonders God had wrought among the Gentiles by them.

Thirdly, this assembly decided the question submitted to it, not by inspiration, but after discussion; and, as would appear, under the ordinary guidance of the Holy Spirit.

Acts 15:7, 22, 28 — And when there had been much disputing, Peter rose up, and said unto them, Men *and* brethren, ye know how that a good while ago God made choice among us, that the Gentiles by my mouth should hear the word of the gospel, and believe...Then pleased it the apostles and elders, with the whole church, to send chosen men of their own company to Antioch with Paul and Barnabas; *namely*, Judas surnamed Barsabas, and Silas, chief men among the brethren... For it seemed good to the Holy Ghost, and to us, to lay upon you no greater burden than these necessary things...

Fourthly, we find that, in this assembly, one member proposed a resolution which was unanimously adopted as the opinion of the whole body.

Acts 15:19, 22 — Wherefore my sentence is, that we trouble not them, which from among the Gentiles are turned to God... Then pleased it the apostles and elders, with the whole church, to send chosen men of their own company to Antioch with Paul and Barnabas; *namely*, Judas surnamed Barsabas, and Silas, chief men among the brethren...

Fifthly, the decision which was thus made was authoritative, extended to all the churches, and was sent down to them and read in them.

Acts 15:28 — For it seemed good to the Holy Ghost, and to us, to lay upon you no greater burden than these necessary things...

And, sixthly, the members of this synod were delegated, not by any single individual or prelate, but by the presbytery of Antioch in conjunction with the other churches.

Acts 15:2 — When therefore Paul and Barnabas had no small dissension and disputation with them, they determined that Paul and Barnabas, and certain other of them, should go up to Jerusalem unto the apostles and elders about this question.

197. *But may it not be objected to all this that the brethren, that is, all the people, were present at this council, as well as the presbyters?*

From what we have already seen, it is most certain that but a small part of the believers then in Jerusalem could have met together in any one place, and therefore, that these brethren must have been delegated by the several churches into which these false teachers had entered, to sit in this council for the right ordering and well managing of the matters submitted to its decision.[71]

Section 9
Of the other bodies appointed by the church.

198. *Who has the power of calling these several councils, or church courts, together?*

The right of calling and dissolving all ecclesiastical courts is, by the Head of the church, exclusively vested in church officers.

Matthew 16:19 — And I will give unto thee the keys of the kingdom of heaven: and whatsoever thou shalt bind on earth shall be bound in heaven: and whatsoever thou shalt loose on earth shall be loosed in heaven.

---

[71] See Bastwick's *Utter Routing*, London, 1641, pp. 430-434.

199. *While these are the regular and constitutional courts of the church, is it lawful and proper for the church to appoint other bodies, for the purpose of carrying out its plans, and executing its will?*

These several courts of the church certainly have power to appoint any body, to carry into execution any plans or operations which it is competent for these courts severally to undertake; provided they do not themselves transcend the powers given to them by the constitution or give to these bodies powers greater than they themselves possess.

200. *What bodies of this kind are employed by the several courts of the church?*

There are committees to prepare or finish any assigned business; agents to discharge any specified duty on behalf of the body appointing them; and boards, or committees, to whom is entrusted the management of the various benevolent operations in which the church is engaged.

CHAPTER 5
POWER OF THE CHURCH

Section 1
Of the nature of church power, and the independence of the church from the civil government.

201. *Do the officers of the church possess any authority over its members?*

Every office implies some authority; and a church officer, without power to sustain his office, would be an anomaly [abnormality].

202. *Why is such power necessary to the officers of the church?*

Because the members of the church, as such, are separated from the rest of mankind and profess to believe in Christ; and it is made the duty of church officers to preserve this character of the church.

203. *Is this power clearly ascribed to the officers of the church, in Scripture?*

Yes; obedience is required from all members of the church to those who rule over them in the Lord.

Hebrews 13:17 — Obey them that have the rule over you, and submit yourselves: for they watch for your souls, as they that must give account, that they may do it with joy, and not with grief: for that *is* unprofitable for you.

204. *Is the power, which church officers possess, the type that will affect the civil interests of men?*

No; it is altogether ecclesiastical, and the type that will affect men only in their relation to the church, and to God.

John 18:36 — Jesus answered, My kingdom is not of this world: if my kingdom were of this world, then would my servants fight, that I should not be delivered to the Jews: but now is my kingdom not from hence.

205. *How else may you describe this power of the church?*

It is spiritual, and addressed to the consciences of those who are subject to it, in contrast to the Jewish polity, which was external, carnal, and typical.

Hebrews 13:17 — Obey them that have the rule over you, and submit yourselves: for they watch for your souls, as they that must give account, that they may do it with joy, and not with grief: for that *is* unprofitable for you.
2 Corinthians 10:4, 5 — (For the weapons of our warfare *are* not carnal, but mighty through God to the pulling down of strong holds;) Casting down imaginations, and every high thing that exalteth itself against the knowledge of God, and bringing into captivity every thought to the obedience of Christ...

206. *In what respects is this power, or government of the church, spiritual?*

Its objects are spiritual; namely, the souls and consciences of men. Its end is spiritual; namely, the glory of God, in the instruction, guidance, and salvation of men. Its law is spiritual; namely, the word of Christ, in its institutions, commands, prohibitions, and promises. Its acts and exercises are spiritual; namely, the admission, exclusion, or discipline of its members. And its sanctions are spiritual; namely, the withdrawment of spiritual privileges and the threatening of the future and everlasting retribution at the hand of the Judge.

See Luke 17:21; Hebrews 9:10, 14; and 8:10; Jeremiah 31:33; Hebrews 7:16, 18.

207. *To what does the power of the officers of the church extend?*

It belongs to them, ministerially, to determine controversies of faith, and cases of conscience; to set down rules and directions for the better ordering of the public worship of God and government of his church; to receive complaints in cases of mal-administration and authoritatively to determine them; and, generally, to devise such plans as will best advance the interests of the kingdom of Christ.

208. *What are the means, which are employed by church officers, for the maintenance of this spiritual power?*

The means employed by church officers to secure this obedience are commands, entreaties, promises, threatenings, and censures; which are all intended to affect the heart only, and not the property, liberty, or personal security of the members of church.

209. *Does the very word "power", as applied to any office in the church, imply that he who exercises it is himself under the authority of a superior?*

Yes; *power* implies the execution of superior orders, by one who is subordinate to that superior.

Matthew 23:8-10 — But be not ye called Rabbi: for one is your Master, *even* Christ; and all ye are brethren. And call no *man* your father upon the earth: for one is your Father, which is in heaven. Neither be ye called masters: for one is your Master, *even* Christ.

210. *In what sense do church officers possess authority?*

By right of the Lord Jesus Christ whom they represent, and who is sole Master in the church.

Matthew 17:5 — While he yet spake, behold, a bright cloud overshadowed them: and behold a voice out of the cloud, which said, This is my beloved Son, in whom I am well pleased; hear ye him.

211. *Have church officers any power or authority, even in ecclesiastical matters, independently, or in themselves considered?*

None whatever; they act altogether ministerially.

Philippians 1:1 — Paul and Timotheus, the servants of Jesus Christ, to all the saints in Christ Jesus which are at Philippi, with the bishops and deacons…
2 Corinthians 4:5 — For we preach not ourselves, but Christ Jesus the Lord; and ourselves your servants for Jesus' sake.
See also Acts 16:4; 15:15-31; Matthew 18:17, 18, 19, 29.

212. *What is the source and limit of all ecclesiastical authority?*

The word of God, to which it is subjected, and by which it is restrained.

Isaiah 8:20 — To the law and to the testimony: if they speak not according to this word, *it is* because *there is* no light in them.
Matthew 28:19, 20 — Go ye therefore, and teach all nations, baptizing them in the name of the Father, and of the Son, and of the Holy Ghost: Teaching them to observe all things whatsoever I have commanded you: and, lo, I am with you alway, *even* unto the end of the world. Amen.
See also Matthew 4:4.

213. *What is the end, for which all such authority is committed to the church?*

The apostle Paul declares it to have been given for edification, and not for destruction.

2 Corinthians 8:10 — And herein I give *my* advice: for this is expedient for you, who have begun before, not only to do, but also to be forward a year ago.
2 Corinthians 13:10 — Therefore I write these things being absent, lest being present I should use sharpness, according to the power which the Lord hath given me to edification, and not to destruction.

214. *What is the name given to that opinion which maintains that the church possesses no power, and that the office of its rulers consists solely in instruction and persuading the people?*

It is called Erastianism from Erastus, its author, a physician who lived in the sixteenth century.

215. *Do Presbyterians ascribe any power to the church which interferes with the authority of the state?*

No; Presbyterians maintain that the church is independent of the state, and distinct from it.

216. *Is the Christian church, then, entirely independent of the civil government?*

Yes; so far as it regards the laws, officers, and duties of the church, it has an inalienable[72] right to an unrestrained and independent jurisdiction in all things sacred; so that, as the church cannot interfere with the civil power in the management of civil concerns, neither can

---

[72] Originally, *indefeasible* [Ed.].

the civil power interfere with the church in the supervision and control of all things sacred.

217. What, then, is the duty of the state to the church?

Civil magistrates may not assume to themselves the administration of the word and sacraments, or in the least interfere in matters of faith; yet, as nursing-fathers, it is their duty to protect the church of our common Lord, without giving the preference to any denomination of Christians above the rest, in such a manner that all ecclesiastical persons whatever, shall enjoy the full, free, and unquestioned liberty of discharging every part of the sacred functions without violence or danger. And, as Jesus Christ has appointed a regular government and discipline in his church, no law of any commonwealth should interfere with, stop, or hinder[73] the due exercise thereof, among the voluntary members of any denomination of Christians, according to their own profession and belief. It is the duty of civil magistrates to protect the person and good name of all their people in such an effectual manner as that no person be suffered, either upon pretense of religion or infidelity, to offer any indignity, violence, abuse, or injury to any other person whatsoever; and to see[74] that all religious and ecclesiastical assemblies be held without molestation or disturbance.

John 18:36; Malachi 2:7; Acts 5:29; Isaiah 49:23; Psalm 105:15; Acts 18:14-16.

218. What is the duty of the church to the state?

It is the duty of the church to pray for all in authority; to respect their persons; to pay them all just tribute and other dues; to obey their lawful commands; and to be subject to their authority for conscience's sake. It is also the duty of the church to preach the Gospel to all men, including those who are in authority; to bear witness for Christ; to assert the authority of his laws, and to require obedience to them.

Romans 13:1-7; Acts 25:10, 11; Tit. 3:1; 1 Peter 2:13-17.

219. Is this power of the church of great importance to be known and preserved?

Yes; this independent and spiritual jurisdiction of the church cannot be abandoned, without sacrificing the honor of Christ, the glory of his kingdom, the very constitution and being of the church, and all liberty, civil and religious.[75]

---

[73] Originally, *with, let, or hinder* [Ed.]

[74] Original, *to take order* [Ed.]

[75] Civil and religious liberty depend upon the fact, that the province of the civil power is entirely separate and distinct from that of the ecclesiastical and cannot, therefore, rightly, and ought not, in any case, be made to interfere with each other.

220. *How may this spiritual authority and independence of the church be violated or lost?*

The spiritual authority and independence of the church may be lost by yielding to any usurpation [taking over] of ecclesiastical power by the civil authorities, or to any ecclesiastical dominion which dispenses with Christ's laws, or assumes his authority. Such usurpation we are therefore, to resist, if needs be, even unto blood, as derogatory to the supremacy and glory of Christ.

Hebrews 2:8, 10; Galatians 4:7; 2 Corinthians 4:4; 1 John 2:16, 17, 22; Revelation 17:8, 11; 2 Thessalonians 2:3, 4; Matthew 12:30; Colossians 2:10, 19; Matthew 4:24.

221. *Do Presbyterians desire, then, any alliance between their church and the state?*

On the contrary, they believe, that any such alliance ever has been, and ever will be, equally injurious to the State and to the church; and that it is to be disapproved[76] by every Christian as the evil[77] source of corruption and intolerance.

Section 2
Of true liberty of conscience.

222. *Can church officers enact any thing contrary or in addition to the word of God and make it binding on the conscience?*

No; God alone is Lord of the conscience and has left it free from the doctrines and commandments of men which are in any thing contrary to his word, or beside it, in matters of faith or worship.

Romans 14:4 — Who art thou that judgest another man's servant? to his own master he standeth or falleth. Yea, he shall be holden up: for God is able to make him stand.

223. *Is it proper for any ecclesiastical officers to require implicit faith in anything for which no scriptural warrant can be given; or an absolute obedience to mere ecclesiastical decrees without such plain warrant?*

No; this is to destroy liberty of conscience, and reason also.

Isaiah 8:20 — To the law and to the testimony: if they speak not according to this word, *it is* because *there is* no light in them.
Acts 17:11 — These were more noble than those in Thessalonica, in that they received the word with all readiness of mind, and searched the scriptures daily, whether those things were so.
John 4:22 — Ye worship ye know not what: we know what we worship: for salvation is of the Jews.
Hosea 5:11 — Ephraim *is* oppressed *and* broken in judgment, because he willingly walked after the commandment.
Revelation 13:12, 16, 17 — And he exerciseth all the power of the first beast before him, and causeth the earth and them which dwell therein to worship the first beast, whose deadly wound was healed... And he causeth all, both small and great, rich and poor, free and bond, to receive a mark in their right hand, or in their foreheads: And that no man might buy or sell, save he that had the mark, or the name of the beast, or the number of his name.

---

[76] Original, *deprecated* [Ed.].
[77] Original, *baneful* [Ed.].

224. *Ought any man, out of conscience, to believe any such doctrines, or to obey any such commandments?* *[i.e., as mentioned in Questions 222 & 223]*

No; to do so would betray their liberty of conscience.

Colossians 2:20, 22, 23 — Wherefore if ye be dead with Christ from the rudiments of the world, why, as though living in the world, are ye subject to ordinances... Which all are to perish with the using;) after the commandments and doctrines of men? Which things have indeed a shew of wisdom in will worship, and humility, and neglecting of the body; not in any honour to the satisfying of the flesh.
Galatians 1:10 — For do I now persuade men, or God? or do I seek to please men? for if I yet pleased men, I should not be the servant of Christ.
Galatians 2:4 — And that because of false brethren unawares brought in, who came in privily to spy out our liberty which we have in Christ Jesus, that they might bring us into bondage...
Galatians 5:1 — Stand fast therefore in the liberty wherewith Christ hath made us free, and be not entangled again with the yoke of bondage.

225. *Does liberty of conscience mean a liberty to transgress or neglect any of God's commandments?*

No; that would be licentiousness, and not liberty.

226. *Does liberty of conscience mean freedom from all obedience to the authority of church officers, as far as they administer faithfully the laws of Christ?*

No; they who oppose any lawful power, or the lawful exercise of it, whether it be ecclesiastical or civil, resist the ordinance of God.

1 Peter 2:13, 14, 16 — Submit yourselves to every ordinance of man for the Lord's sake: whether it be to the king, as supreme; Or unto governors, as unto them that are sent by him for the punishment of evildoers, and for the praise of them that do well... As free, and not using *your* liberty for a cloke of maliciousness, but as the servants of God.
See also Hebrews 13:17, Romans 13:1, 8.

227. *What, then, do you mean by liberty of conscience?*

True liberty of conscience is freedom from the enforcement of any doctrine or commandment of men, that is in any thing contrary to the general rules of God's word, or beside[78] it, if matters of faith or worship.[79]

Acts 4:19 — But Peter and John answered and said unto them, Whether it be right in the sight of God to hearken unto you more than unto God, judge ye.
Acts 5:29 — Then Peter and the *other* apostles answered and said, We ought to obey God rather than men. *(cont'd)*

---

[78] *beside* meaning *not explicitly warranted* [Ed.]

[79] Original, *general rules of God's word, or beside it, either in (not "if") matters of faith or worship* was a virtual quoting by the author of Westminster Confession 20.2, which had been slightly, but not insignificantly corrupted over the years as exposed by the discovery of the 1646 assembly original Cornelius Burges manuscript discovered in the early twentieth century (see *The Confession of Faith of the Assembly of Divines at Westminster from the original manuscript written by Cornelius Burges in 1646* edited by S. W. Carruthers, M.D., Ph.D. (Edin.) London, 1946). Confer also with 1995 edition of Westminster Confession of Faith by Free Presbyterian Publications, p. 86 in contrast to earlier editions p. 86. The assumption is that if the author had known of this error, he would have written the question as indicated above. [Ed.]

1 **Corinthians 7:23** — Ye are bought with a price; be not ye the servants of men.
Matthew 23:8, 10 — But be not ye called Rabbi: for one is your Master, *even* Christ; and all ye are brethren... Neither be ye called masters: for one is your Master, *even* Christ.
2 Corinthians 1:24 — Not for that we have dominion over your faith, but are helpers of your joy: for by faith ye stand.
Matthew 15:9 — But in vain they do worship me, teaching *for* doctrines the commandments of men.

228. ***Can any article of faith be believed, on any other authority than that of the written word of God?***

It cannot; for it is not given to any man, even were he an apostle, to exercise dominion over our faith; while a curse is pronounced upon any man, who will either add to, or take from, this book.

2 Corinthians 1:24 — Not for that we have dominion over your faith, but are helpers of your joy: for by faith ye stand.
Revelation 22:19 — And if any man shall take away from the words of the book of this prophecy, God shall take away his part out of the book of life, and out of the holy city, and *from* the things which are written in this book.

Section 3
Of the divisions of church power
— and first of its dogmatic power.[80]

229. *What are the different parts of the power of the church?*

The power of the church is commonly divided, according to the nature of the objects about which it is employed, into three parts.

230. *What is the first part of the power of the church?*

That which is called dogmatic, or which respects articles of faith.

231. *Has the church power to make such articles?*

All Protestants agree in believing that the Scriptures contain all the truths which it is necessary for man to know; and that they constitute the only infallible rule of faith.

232. *What other rule does the church of Rome adopt?*

The church of Rome adopts another rule of faith, called *tradition*; by which she means a summary of doctrine which is in the possession of the church, besides that contained in Scripture, and which is of equal authority with the Scriptures themselves.

233. *Is there any foundation for this doctrine of tradition in the word of God?*

The Scriptures, on the contrary, denounce the severest anathema [cursed thing] upon any who will add to, or take from, the written word of God. *(cont'd)*

---

[80] i.e., the power to write a confession of faith which contains dogma (doctrine) or to state and define biblical faith [Ed.].

Revelation 22:18, 19 — For I testify unto every man that heareth the words of the prophecy of this book, If any man shall add unto these things, God shall add unto him the plagues that are written in this book: And if any man shall take away from the words of the book of this prophecy, God shall take away his part out of the book of life, and out of the holy city, and *from* the things which are written in this book.

Galatians 1:9 — As we said before, so say I now again, If any *man* preach any other gospel unto you than that ye have received, let him be accursed.

See also Deuteronomy 4:2, 12, 32; Proverbs 30:6; Isaiah 8:20; Matthew 15:3-6; Colossians 2:8.

234. **What had been the result of the adoption of tradition, as a standard of doctrine, in the church of Rome?**

It has introduced into the creed of that church human dogmas[81], and grossly erroneous tenets [doctrines]; for which she demands implicit reception, under pain of being accursed.

235. **What, then, is the power of the church, as it regards the Scriptures?**

The church is the depository of the Scriptures; and bound to preserve them, pure and unadulterated.

1 Timothy 3:15 — But if I tarry long, that thou mayest know how thou oughtest to behave thyself in the house of God, which is the church of the living God, the pillar and ground of the truth.

236. **What further power has the church, in reference to the Scriptures?**

It is the duty of the church to explain the Scriptures, and to call upon all men to study, believe, and obey them for themselves.

Malachi 2:7 — For the priest's lips should keep knowledge, and they should seek the law at his mouth: for he *is* the messenger of the LORD of hosts.

Isaiah 8:20 — To the law and to the testimony: if they speak not according to this word, *it is* because *there is* no light in them.

John 5:39 —Search the scriptures; for in them ye think ye have eternal life: and they are they which testify of me.

See also 2 Timothy 3:15; Colossians 3:16.

Romans 15:4 — For whatsoever things were written aforetime were written for our learning, that we through patience and comfort of the scriptures might have hope.

Acts 17:11 — These were more noble than those in Thessalonica, in that they received the word with all readiness of mind, and searched the scriptures daily, whether those things were so.

Section 4
Of confessions of faith.

237. **Has the church the right to draw up summaries of Christian doctrines; as, for instance, confessions of faith and catechisms?**

In order to exhibit to the world her views of the Scriptures; to oppose prevailing heresies and errors; to instruct her children and people; to determine the sentiments of candidates for admission into the ministry; and to secure harmony and uniformity in her public ministry; it is the privilege and duty of every church, to draw up such summaries of Christian doctrine.

---

[81] *Human dogmas* being those doctrines invented by men, rather than derived from Scripture [Ed.].

238. What authority do these summaries possess, in themselves considered?

They have, in themselves considered, no more authority than any other human compositions.

239. From what, then, is their authority derived?

The authority of such summaries is derived solely from their conformity to the Scriptures.

240. Are such summaries to be regarded as infallibly correct?

No; the only *infallible* rule for the interpretation of Scripture, is Scripture itself.

Romans 12:6 — Having then gifts differing according to the grace that is given to us, whether prophecy, *let us prophesy* according to the proportion of faith...
John 5:46 — For had ye believed Moses, ye would have believed me: for he wrote of me.

241. Does our confession of faith claim any other power over those who receive it?

No; for it is stated in that confession that *all synods or councils, since the apostles' times, may err, and many have erred; therefore, they are not to be made the rule of faith or practice, but to be used as a help to both.*

See Westminster Confession of Faith *31:4 (U.S. edition, 31:3).*

242. Can you state any other declaration which that confession makes of the same significance[82]?

Yes; it declares that "it belongeth to synods and councils *ministerially,* (that is, as minister of God's word,) to determine controversies of faith and cases of conscience;" and that their "decrees and determination, *if consonant to the word of God,* are to be received with reverence and submission."

See Westminster Confession of Faith *31:3 (U.S. edition, 31:2). See also chapters 1, 9, 10 and 20 at large.*

243. How, then, do you reconcile the authority claimed for these standards with that supreme authority which is ascribed to the word of God?

No individual is compelled to receive these standards, contrary to his own voluntary choice; and in submitting himself to the authority of the church, every individual declares that he receives its standards, *because,* after full examination, he believes them to contain the system of doctrine taught in the Holy Scriptures.

See Presbyterian Church of the United States Form of Government, *chapter xv. 12.*[83]

---

[82] Originally, *purport* [Ed.].

[83] These locations will vary in other Presbyterian denominations and may differ to greater or lesser degrees. [Ed.]

244. *You have said, that no individual is required to adopt these standards; will you now inform me whether any individual who may have adopted them, is at liberty, should he see fit, to withdraw his declaration of full belief in them?*

Should any individual be led to regard any part of these standards as contrary to the word of God, it is his privilege and duty to release himself[84] from that obligation; or otherwise, as a man of honor, to maintain and defend them so long as he continues to act as a minister or elder of the church.

245. *Is there any thing in this to interfere with true liberty of conscience?*

Nothing; for while such a course is adapted to secure peace and harmony, and united action, it also preserves and maintains true liberty of conscience.

246. *Who are required explicitly to adopt and promise obedience to the standards of the church?*

Bishops [pastors], licentiates, elders and deacons.[85]

See Presbyterian Church of the United States Form of Government, *chap. 15:12, chap. 14:7, and chap 13:4.*[86]

Section 5
Of the second part of the power of the church,
to enact rules for its government or order.

247. *What is the second part of the power of the church?*

The power to enact rules for its government or order.

248. *Does this mean, that the church has power to establish any form of government which shall appear most eligible?*

No; as far as there is a particular form laid down in Scripture, that form cannot be altered without usurping the authority of Jesus Christ.

Hebrews 8:5 — Who serve unto the example and shadow of heavenly things, as Moses was admonished of God when he was about to make the tabernacle: for, See, saith he, *that* thou make all things according to the pattern shewed to thee in the mount.

---

[84] This would require him to resign from the ministry in association with the Presbyterian Church should his beliefs become contrary to the Westminster Confession of Faith.

[85] The same standards are not generally required of members, as that of officers because these standards were written with a theological expertise expected of officers. If members were expected to have the same knowledge, the church would only be suitable for intellectuals. [Ed.]

[86] These locations will vary in other Presbyterian denominations and may differ to greater or lesser degrees. [Ed.]

249. *Does this mean, that the church has power to make new laws to regulate the moral conduct of its members?*

The church, as we have already shown, has no legislative but only ministerial authority; and her office consists SOLELY in publishing and enforcing those laws which the Head of the church has already enacted.

250. *Has the church power to decree rites and ceremonies, as is taught in the articles of the Church of Rome, and of the Protestant Episcopal Church?*

There is no scriptural warrant whatever for this opinion; and we, therefore, believe that the church assumes a power which does not belong to her when she makes any addition to the institutions of Christ and requires their observance on pain of censure or excommunication.[87]

251. *What other matters come under this power of the church, to enact rules for government and order?*

It belongs to the church to appoint the times of public worship, and on what other occasions its members shall join in the solemn exercises of religion.

252. *Are there any other matters included under this power of enacting rules?*

It is also the responsibility[88] of the church to point out the order of public worship, to fix the bounds of congregations and presbyteries, and to make all other arrangements, which are necessary to secure harmony and order.

Section 6
Of the third division of the power of the church, or the power of discipline.

253. *What is the third and last part of ecclesiastical power?*

The power of discipline or jurisdiction.

2 Corinthians 10:8 — For though I should boast somewhat more of our authority, which the Lord hath given us for edification, and not for your destruction, I should not be ashamed...

254. *Is this power necessary to every society?*

Yes; in every society of men, some power is necessary to preserve the common peace and to maintain concord.

---

[87] For a notice of some of the objectionable results of the exercise of this power, see chap. 7, sect. 2, Question and Answer 304.

[88] Original, *province* [Ed.].

255. *Has any person a right to admission into the Christian church, without regard to its rules or regulations?*

No; only those who make a credible profession of their faith in Christ can be admitted as members of the church of Christ.

Acts 8:37 — And Philip said, If thou believest with all thine heart, thou mayest. And he answered and said, I believe that Jesus Christ is the Son of God.
1 Corinthians 1:2 — Unto the church of God which is at Corinth, to them that are sanctified in Christ Jesus, called *to be* saints, with all that in every place call upon the name of Jesus Christ our Lord, both theirs and ours...
Matthew 28:20 — Teaching them to observe all things whatsoever I have commanded you: and, lo, I am with you alway, *even* unto the end of the world. Amen.

256. *Why may not others, also, be admitted into the church?*

Because its privileges, by their very nature, are intended only for those who, in the judgment of charity, are disciples of Christ.

John 17:6 — I have manifested thy name unto the men which thou gavest me out of the world: thine they were, and thou gavest them me; and they have kept thy word.
Acts 19:9 — But when divers were hardened, and believed not, but spake evil of that way before the multitude, he departed from them, and separated the disciples, disputing daily in the school of one Tyrannus.

257. *By what means is the character of the church, as a society of professing Christians, to be preserved?*

By faithful exercise of a scriptural discipline, in enforcing the observance of her laws, and by censure and excommunication.

1 Corinthians 5:7 — Purge out therefore the old leaven, that ye may be a new lump, as ye are unleavened. For even Christ our passover is sacrificed for us... (see context)

258. *Why is this exercise of discipline necessary to the purity and peace of the church?*

Because offenses will frequently arise from unregenerate professors,[89] and from the remaining corruptions of those who are truly pious.

Matthew 18:7 — Woe unto the world because of offences! for it must needs be that offences come; but woe to that man by whom the offence cometh!
Revelation 2:14 — But I have a few things against thee, because thou hast there them that hold the doctrine of Balaam, who taught Balac to cast a stumblingblock before the children of Israel, to eat things sacrificed unto idols, and to commit fornication.

259. *Who are to exercise this discipline?*

The officers of the church.

Matthew 28:19. Acts 14:23. Matthew 16:19 — And I will give unto thee the keys of the kingdom of heaven: and whatsoever thou shalt bind on earth shall be bound in heaven: and whatsoever thou shalt loose on earth shall be loosed in heaven.
Matthew 18:15-18 — Moreover if thy brother shall trespass against thee, go and tell him his fault between thee and him alone: if he shall hear thee, thou hast gained thy brother. But if he will not hear *thee, then* take with thee one or two more, that in the mouth of two or three witnesses every word may be established. And if he shall neglect to hear them, tell *it* unto the church: but if he neglect to hear the church, let him be unto thee as an heathen man

---

[89] those who profess faith in Christ [Ed.]

and a publican. Verily I say unto you, Whatsoever ye shall bind on earth shall be bound in heaven: and whatsoever ye shall loose on earth shall be loosed in heaven.

260. *How far does this power of church officers extend?*

It is their responsibility[90] to judge who may be admitted to the church; to inspect their conduct when received; and to censure and expel such as prove to be unworthy.

2 Timothy 4:2 — Preach the word; be instant in season, out of season; reprove, rebuke, exhort with all longsuffering and doctrine.
Titus 2:15 — These things speak, and exhort, and rebuke with all authority. Let no man despise thee.
1 Corinthians 5:12 — For what have I to do to judge them also that are without? do not ye judge them that are within?
Hebrews 13:17 — Obey them that have the rule over you, and submit yourselves: for they watch for your souls, as they that must give account, that they may do it with joy, and not with grief: for that *is* unprofitable for you.

Section 7
Of admission to, and exclusion from, the church.

261. *Are only those who are really saints, to be admitted into the church?*

That any man is *really* a saint, can be known only to God; and, therefore, the officers of the church, not having knowledge to discern the heart, cannot determine the secret state of the soul.

262. *By what rule, then, are they to be guided in the reception of members into the church?*

They are to be guided solely by the outward profession which is made, of inward faith in Christ Jesus.

Acts 8:12 — But when they believed Philip preaching the things concerning the kingdom of God, and the name of Jesus Christ, they were baptized, both men and women.
Acts 19:18 — And many that believed came, and confessed, and shewed their deeds.

263. *When is a person to be regarded as making a credible profession of Christianity?*

When such an individual manifests an acquaintance with the leading doctrines of the Gospel; declares himself a believer in them; professes that his heart has been renewed by the Spirit of God; and maintains a conduct becoming[91] the Gospel.

Romans 10:10 — For with the heart man believeth unto righteousness; and with the mouth confession is made unto salvation.
Acts 16:33 — And he took them the same hour of the night, and washed *their* stripes; and was baptized, he and all his, straightway.
Luke 3:8 — Bring forth therefore fruits worthy of repentance, and begin not to say within yourselves, We have Abraham to *our* father: for I say unto you, That God is able of these stones to raise up children unto Abraham.

---

[90] Original, *province* [Ed.].
[91] suitable or agreeable to [Ed.]

264. *Do the members of the church, after their admission to it, continue subject to the authority of its rulers?*

Yes. Such authority on the one part, and obedience on the other, are most plainly sanctioned by the law of Christ.

See 1 Corinthians 5:12, 13; Hebrews 13:17.

265. *For what offenses are members of the church liable to its censure?*

For errors in doctrine; for immorality in practice; for despising the authority, order, or ordinances of the church; and for neglecting the public, domestic, and secret duties of religion.

Romans 16:17 — Now I beseech you, brethren, mark them which cause divisions and offences contrary to the doctrine which ye have learned; and avoid them.

Titus 3:10 — A man that is an heretick after the first and second admonition reject...

2 Chronicles 23:19 — And he set the porters at the gates of the house of the LORD, that none *which was* unclean in any thing should enter in.

Ephesians 5:11 — And have no fellowship with the unfruitful works of darkness, but rather reprove *them*.

1 Corinthians 5:11 — But now I have written unto you not to keep company, if any man that is called a brother be a fornicator, or covetous, or an idolater, or a railer, or a drunkard, or an extortioner; with such an one no not to eat.

Revelation 2:20 — Notwithstanding I have a few things against thee, because thou sufferest that woman Jezebel, which calleth herself a prophetess, to teach and to seduce my servants to commit fornication, and to eat things sacrificed unto idols.

1 Corinthians 11:12 — For as the woman *is* of the man, even so *is* the man also by the woman; but all things of God.

2 Thessalonians 3:6 — Now we command you, brethren, in the name of our Lord Jesus Christ, that ye withdraw yourselves from every brother that walketh disorderly, and not after the tradition which he received of us.

Hebrews 10:25 — Not forsaking the assembling of ourselves together, as the manner of some *is*; but exhorting *one another*: and so much the more, as ye see the day approaching.

Jeremiah 10:25 — Pour out thy fury upon the heathen that know thee not, and upon the families that call not on thy name: for they have eaten up Jacob, and devoured him, and consumed him, and have made his habitation desolate.

Matthew 6:6 — But thou, when thou prayest, enter into thy closet, and when thou hast shut thy door, pray to thy Father which is in secret; and thy Father which seeth in secret shall reward thee openly.

266. *Are all offenses to be followed by the same degree of censure?*

No; according to the nature of the offense[92], some should be rebuked, others suspended from the privileges of the church, and others excommunicated, or entirely cut off from all connection with the church.

Titus 1:13 — This witness is true. Wherefore rebuke them sharply, that they may be sound in the faith...

2 Thessalonians 3:14, 15 — And if any man obey not our word by this epistle, note that man, and have no company with him, that he may be ashamed. Yet count *him* not as an enemy, but admonish *him* as a brother.

1 Corinthians 5:13 — But them that are without God judgeth. Therefore put away from among yourselves that wicked person.

Galatians 5:12 — I would they were even cut off which trouble you.

See also 1 Timothy 5:20.

---

[92] Original, *their several offenses* [Ed.].

267. *Do the Scriptures attach a very solemn importance to the censures of the church?*

They do; for they declare that the sentence of the church, when pronounced according to the Scriptures, is confirmed and ratified in heaven.

Matthew 18:18 — Verily I say unto you, Whatsoever ye shall bind on earth shall be bound in heaven: and whatsoever ye shall loose on earth shall be loosed in heaven.
1 Corinthians 5:5 — To deliver such an one unto Satan for the destruction of the flesh, that the spirit may be saved in the day of the Lord Jesus.
1 Timothy 1:20 — Of whom is Hymenaeus and Alexander; whom I have delivered unto Satan, that they may learn not to blaspheme.

268. *What should be the conduct of those who have been, in either of these ways, subjected to the discipline of the church?*

They should humble themselves under it; and seek grace to repent and do their first works.[93]

1 Peter 5:6 — Humble yourselves therefore under the mighty hand of God, that he may exalt you in due time...
Hebrews 13:17 — Obey them that have the rule over you, and submit yourselves: for they watch for your souls, as they that must give account, that they may do it with joy, and not with grief: for that *is* unprofitable for you.
Revelation 2:5 — Remember therefore from whence thou art fallen, and repent, and do the first works; or else I will come unto thee quickly, and will remove thy candlestick out of his place, except thou repent.

269. *When may a person who has been suspended be restored to the communion of the church?*

Whenever sufficient evidence has been provided[94] of his repentance and reformation.

Galatians 6:1 — Brethren, if a man be overtaken in a fault, ye which are spiritual, restore such an one in the spirit of meekness; considering thyself, lest thou also be tempted.
John 20:23 — Whose soever sins ye remit, they are remitted unto them; *and* whose soever *sins* ye retain, they are retained.

270. *Are any censures of the church to be made public?*

Yes; when the offenses are of such magnitude and publicity as to bring scandal upon the church.

2 Corinthians 2:6 — Sufficient to such a man *is* this punishment, which *was inflicted* of many.
1 Timothy 5:20 — Them that sin rebuke before all, that others also may fear.

271. *Is the church injured by the neglect of discipline?*

Yes; for thereby godly persons will be deterred from entering it; the anger of God provoked; and Christ's name dishonored.

1 Corinthians 5:11 — But now I have written unto you not to keep company, if any man that is called a brother be a fornicator, or covetous, or an idolater, or a railer, or a drunkard, or an extortioner; with such an one no not to eat.   *(cont'd)*

---

[93] *First works*, meaning *primary* or *most basic works* [Ed.]
[94] Original, *afforded* [Ed.].

1 Corinthians 10:20 — But I *say*, that the things which the Gentiles sacrifice, they sacrifice to devils, and not to God: and I would not that ye should have fellowship with devils.

Revelation 18:4 — And I heard another voice from heaven, saying, Come out of her, my people, that ye be not partakers of her sins, and that ye receive not of her plagues.

Jeremiah 7:11 — Is this house, which is called by my name, become a den of robbers in your eyes? Behold, even I have seen *it*, saith the LORD.

2 Samuel 12:14 — Howbeit, because by this deed thou hast given great occasion to the enemies of the LORD to blaspheme, the child also *that is* born unto thee shall surely die.

Romans 2:24 — For the name of God is blasphemed among the Gentiles through you, as it is written.

Ephesians 4:30 — And grieve not the holy Spirit of God, whereby ye are sealed unto the day of redemption.

272. *May a church, by the utter neglect of discipline, cease to be a true and living church of Christ?*

Yes; this has happened.

Revelation 2:9 — I know thy works, and tribulation, and poverty, (but thou art rich) and *I know* the blasphemy of them which say they are Jews, and are not, but *are* the synagogue of Satan.

Revelation 3:9, 16 — Behold, I will make them of the synagogue of Satan, which say they are Jews, and are not, but do lie; behold, I will make them to come and worship before thy feet, and to know that I have loved thee... So then because thou art lukewarm, and neither cold nor hot, I will spue thee out of my mouth.

273. *On the other hand, are there many and great benefits arising from the exercise of strict and faithful discipline?*

Yes.

274. *What benefits may arise to the offender from the exercise of discipline?*

By this he sees sin to be evil and shameful; and if he receive the censure in a proper spirit, it has a powerful tendency to humble, reclaim, and edify him.

2 Thessalonians 3:4 — And we have confidence in the Lord touching you, that ye both do and will do the things which we command you.

2 Corinthians 7:9, 10 — Now I rejoice, not that ye were made sorry, but that ye sorrowed to repentance: for ye were made sorry after a godly manner, that ye might receive damage by us in nothing. For godly sorrow worketh repentance to salvation not to be repented of: but the sorrow of the world worketh death.

275. *What benefits arise to the church from the faithful exercise of discipline?*

By it, sinners are discouraged from hypocritically joining the church, and the leaven which might infect the whole lump is purged out; the number of her true converts is increased, her holiness is manifested; the honor of the Head is vindicated; and God's gracious presence and blessing secured.

1 Corinthians 5:7 — Purge out therefore the old leaven, that ye may be a new lump, as ye are unleavened. For even Christ our passover is sacrificed for us...

Acts 16:4, 5 — And as they went through the cities, they delivered them the decrees for to keep, that were ordained of the apostles and elders which were at Jerusalem. And so were the churches established in the faith, and increased in number daily.

Acts 5:11, 13, 14 — And great fear came upon all the church, and upon as many as heard these things... And of the rest durst no man join himself to them: but the people magnified them. And believers were the more added to the Lord, multitudes both of men and women.)

John 2:16 — And said unto them that sold doves, Take these things hence; make not my Father's house an house of merchandise.

Ezekiel 36:23 — And I will sanctify my great name, which was profaned among the heathen, which ye have profaned in the midst of them; and the heathen shall know that I *am* the LORD, saith the Lord GOD, when I shall be sanctified in you before their eyes.

2 Corinthians 6:17, 18 — Wherefore come out from among them, and be ye separate, saith the Lord, and touch not the unclean *thing*; and I will receive you, 18 And will be a Father unto you, and ye shall be my sons and daughters, saith the Lord Almighty.

276. But may not the offender, by the exercise of discipline, be led to forsake the preaching of the Gospel, and thus become more hardened?

As discipline is an ordinance of God, we must expect the *neglect* rather than the *exercise* of it to harden the sinner; but if, in his pride and obstinacy, he disregards the advantages which flow from it when received in a right spirit, the rulers of the church are not to be deterred from their duty, any more than the minister of the Gospel from preaching because many are hardened by it and have their guilt and dangers increased.

2 Corinthians 2:15 — For we are unto God a sweet savour of Christ, in them that are saved, and in them that perish...

Jude 19 — These be they who separate themselves, sensual, having not the Spirit.

277. Are the rulers of the church deeply responsible for the right exercise of discipline?

They who hold office by appointment from Christ, whose faithfulness will be followed by so many and great blessings, whose negligence must be the source of such deep and lasting injuries to the church, dishonor to Christ, and evil to sinners; should feel themselves under a most solemn responsibility in this matter, and must expect to be called to a most strict account at the day of judgment, for the part which they act in relation to it.

1 Peter 5:4 — And when the chief Shepherd shall appear, ye shall receive a crown of glory that fadeth not away.

Hebrews 13:17 — Obey them that have the rule over you, and submit yourselves: for they watch for your souls, as they that must give account, that they may do it with joy, and not with grief: for that *is* unprofitable for you.

278. How may each member of the church fully understand all its rules, and order of discipline?

By studying the Form of Government and Book of Discipline attached to the Confession of our Faith and which every member of our church should possess.[95]

---

[95] The government of every Presbyterian Church is contained in its *Form of Government* and *Book of Discipline*, also called today *Book of Church Order*. The original *Form of Government* of the Presbyterian Church was established by the Westminster Assembly in 1645 and was the basis of all Presbyterian Church government.

CHAPTER 6
FELLOWSHIP OF THE CHURCH

Section 1
Of the nature and necessity of church fellowship.

279. *Is a knowledge of the true nature, constitution, and design of the church, important to all its members?*

It is important; for otherwise they will be in ignorance of those duties which they are under obligation to discharge as members of the church.

Ezekiel 44:5, 8 — And the LORD said unto me, Son of man, mark well, and behold with thine eyes, and hear with thine ears all that I say unto thee concerning all the ordinances of the house of the LORD, and all the laws thereof; and mark well the entering in of the house, with every going forth of the sanctuary... And ye have not kept the charge of mine holy things: but ye have set keepers of my charge in my sanctuary for yourselves.
Matthew 5:9 — Blessed *are* the peacemakers: for they shall be called the children of God.

280. *Who are members of the visible church of Christ?*

Those who have been admitted into it on profession of their faith and obedience, together with their children.

Acts 2:38, 39, 47 — Then Peter said unto them, Repent, and be baptized every one of you in the name of Jesus Christ for the remission of sins, and ye shall receive the gift of the Holy Ghost. For the promise is unto you, and to your children, and to all that are afar off, *even* as many as the Lord our God shall call... Praising God, and having favour with all the people. And the Lord added to the church daily such as should be saved.

281. *Is it the duty of all, or only of some, to become members of the church of Christ?*

It is the unquestionable duty of all who hear the Gospel, to believe in the Lord Jesus Christ; and then to become members of his visible church.

Acts 2:38 — Then Peter said unto them, Repent, and be baptized every one of you in the name of Jesus Christ for the remission of sins, and ye shall receive the gift of the Holy Ghost.
Romans 10:9 — That if thou shalt confess with thy mouth the Lord Jesus, and shalt believe in thine heart that God hath raised him from the dead, thou shalt be saved.
1 John 1:3 — That which we have seen and heard declare we unto you, that ye also may have fellowship with us: and truly our fellowship *is* with the Father, and with his Son Jesus Christ.

282. *What are the ends [purposes] of church fellowship?*

The ends of church fellowship are: that Christians may hold forth the doctrines of the Bible; maintain the ordinances of the Gospel uncorrupted; promote their mutual holiness and edification; and thus become fitted for glory.

Colossians 2:2 — That their hearts might be comforted, being knit together in love, and unto all riches of the full assurance of understanding, to the acknowledgement of the mystery of God, and of the Father, and of Christ... *(cont'd)*

See also Revelation 2:25.

Philippians 2:15 — That ye may be blameless and harmless, the sons of God, without rebuke, in the midst of a crooked and perverse nation, among whom ye shine as lights in the world...

Colossians 1:12 — Giving thanks unto the Father, which hath made us meet to be partakers of the inheritance of the saints in light...

283. **What are the privileges of members of the church?**

The participation of the Lord's supper, the baptism of their children; pastoral oversight; the sympathy and prayers of the church; the special promises of God; and the right of deciding upon all matters referred to them relative to the spiritual interests of the church.

Isaiah 4:5, 6 — And the LORD will create upon every dwelling place of mount Zion, and upon her assemblies, a cloud and smoke by day, and the shining of a flaming fire by night: for upon all the glory *shall be* a defence. And there shall be a tabernacle for a shadow in the daytime from the heat, and for a place of refuge, and for a covert from storm and from rain.

1 Timothy 4:10 — For therefore we both labour and suffer reproach, because we trust in the living God, who is the Saviour of all men, specially of those that believe.

Acts 2:42 —And they continued stedfastly in the apostles' doctrine and fellowship, and in breaking of bread, and in prayers.

Psalm 147: 19, 20 — He sheweth his word unto Jacob, his statutes and his judgments unto Israel. He hath not dealt so with any nation: and *as for his* judgments, they have not known them. Praise ye the LORD.

Romans 9:4 — Who are Israelites; to whom *pertaineth* the adoption, and the glory, and the covenants, and the giving of the law, and the service *of God*, and the promises...

Section 2
Of the duties of church members.

284. **What duties do members of the church owe to their pastor?**

They should submit to his just and scriptural authority; love and esteem him; attend constantly upon his ministrations; cooperate with him in every good work; liberally support him; and earnestly pray for him.

1 Thessalonians 5:13 — And to esteem them very highly in love for their work's sake. *And* be at peace among yourselves.

Hebrews 13:7 — Remember them which have the rule over you, who have spoken unto you the word of God: whose faith follow, considering the end of *their* conversation.

See also 1 Corinthians 16:15, 16; 1 Thessalonians 5 :11, 12; 2 Corinthians 1:11.

285. **What duties do the members of the church owe to one another?**

They should love one another; visit each other in affliction; pray for one another; when necessary, exercise forbearance and charity; watch over one another; and endeavor to live in peace and harmony.

Galatians 6:2 — Bear ye one another's burdens, and so fulfil the law of Christ.

James 5:16 — Confess *your* faults one to another, and pray one for another, that ye may be healed. The effectual fervent prayer of a righteous man availeth much.

Ephesians 4:2 — With all lowliness and meekness, with longsuffering, forbearing one another in love...

Romans 12:13 — Distributing to the necessity of saints; given to hospitality.

1 John 3:17 — But whoso hath this world's good, and seeth his brother have need, and shutteth up his bowels *of compassion* from him, how dwelleth the love of God in him? *(cont'd)*

Leviticus 19:17 — Thou shalt not hate thy brother in thine heart: thou shalt in any wise rebuke thy neighbour, and not suffer sin upon him.
See also 1 Peter 5:5; Philippians 2:3.

286. **What duties do members of the church owe to the church itself?**

They are bound to support it; to take a deep and active interest in all its concerns; to seek its prosperity by all lawful means; and cordially to submit to its discipline.

1 Corinthians 16:2 — Upon the first *day* of the week let every one of you lay by him in store, as *God* hath prospered him, that there be no gatherings when I come.

287. **What is the duty of members of the church to themselves, as individuals?**

To grow in knowledge, in grace, and in communion with God; and to lead holy and exemplary lives.

John 5:39 — Search the scriptures; for in them ye think ye have eternal life: and they are they which testify of me.
Psalm 1:2 — But his delight *is* in the law of the LORD; and in his law doth he meditate day and night.

288. **What is the duty of members of the church, as heads of families?**

To maintain family prayer; to set a holy example; and to govern and direct their children and employees[96] in the fear and admonition of the Lord.

Genesis 18:19 — For I know him, that he will command his children and his household after him, and they shall keep the way of the LORD, to do justice and judgment; that the LORD may bring upon Abraham that which he hath spoken of him.
Psalm 118:15 — The voice of rejoicing and salvation *is* in the tabernacles of the righteous: the right hand of the LORD doeth valiantly.
Jeremiah 10:25 — Pour out thy fury upon the heathen that know thee not, and upon the families that call not on thy name: for they have eaten up Jacob, and devoured him, and consumed him, and have made his habitation desolate.
Ephesians 6:4 — And, ye fathers, provoke not your children to wrath: but bring them up in the nurture and admonition of the Lord.

289. **What is the duty of church members, as citizens?**

They should live peaceful, holy, and unblamable lives, in all honesty and fidelity; adorning the doctrines of God our Saviour; and, as far as they are able[97] in them, securing a good report of them that are without.

290. **What is the duty of members of the church, as it regards property?**

They should remember that, in the possession of whatever amount of property they have, they are stewards for God and must render an account to him of the manner in which it has been used for the furtherance of his glory.

2 Corinthians 9: 7; Acts 11:20; Proverbs 3:9; 1 Timothy 6:17; Romans 10:14, 15.

---

[96] Original, *servants* [Ed.].

[97] Original, *lieth* [Ed.]

291. *Is a refusal thus to contribute to the support and spread of the cause of Christ severely reproved in Scripture?*

Yes; it is distinctly said to be a sign of a graceless state; while, on the contrary, liberality is regarded as one evidence of Christian character.

1 John 3:7; 1 Corinthians 6:10; Ephesians 5:5; Proverbs 21: 26; Ezekiel 18:7, 9;. Psalm 112:5, 9; 2 Corinthians 8: 1-8, 24.

CHAPTER 7
RELATION OF THE PRESBYTERIAN CHURCH TO OTHER DENOMINATIONS, AND TO THE WORLD

Section 1
Of Romanism.

292. *Did the church of Christ always continue pure?*

Even from the very time of the apostles, the church was greatly distracted by numberless heresies and superstitions, of the most extravagant description; and the bishops of Rome, pretending to be the successors of the apostle Peter, gradually subjected all the other churches to their control and, at length, showed that they were that antichrist[98] which had been foretold.

See 2 Thessalonians 2:3-7.

293. *When did the church of Christ throw off the yoke of Rome?*

Various churches and individuals attempted, at different times, to throw off the yoke of the church of Rome, some of whom only partially succeeded, while all of them were persecuted, and many destroyed; till, at length, God raised up Luther who, assisted by the German princes, protested against the authority of the pope; and thus, ever since the church of Christ has been a Protestant church.

294. *Is the term Protestant properly applicable to the Presbyterian church?*

It is properly applicable to it, in common with all the other reformed churches.

295. *Why are these all denominated Protestant?*

Because they still adhere to that solemn protest which was made by the reformers of the sixteenth century against the errors and corruptions of the church of Rome.

296. *Name some of those errors and corruptions of the church of Rome, against which the church of Christ has thus protested.*

A. **The church of Rome denies that the Scriptures alone are a sufficient rule of faith and practice.**

> **Isaiah 8:20** — To the law and to the testimony: if they speak not according to this word, *it is* because *there is* no light in them.
> **Acts 17:11** — These were more noble than those in Thessalonica, in that they received the word with all readiness of mind, and searched the scriptures daily, whether those things were so. *(cont'd)*

---

[98] The suggestion here is that they were of that which opposes Christ or presumes to act "instead" of Christ and is called antichrist, not that they were a singular person known as the Antichrist. [Ed.]

2 Timothy 3:16, 17 — All scripture *is* given by inspiration of God, and *is* profitable for doctrine, for reproof, for correction, for instruction in righteousness: That the man of God may be perfect, throughly furnished unto all good works.

John 5:39 — Search the scriptures; for in them ye think ye have eternal life: and they are they which testify of me.

B.   It receives oral traditions as of equal authority in religious matters with the Scriptures; and thus substitutes human authority for the word of God.

Matthew 15:3, 6 — But he answered and said unto them, Why do ye also transgress the commandment of God by your tradition?... And honour not his father or his mother, *he shall be free.* Thus have ye made the commandment of God of none effect by your tradition.

Galatians 1:8 — But though we, or an angel from heaven, preach any other gospel unto you than that which we have preached unto you, let him be accursed.

Colossians 2:8 — Beware lest any man spoil you through philosophy and vain deceit, after the tradition of men, after the rudiments of the world, and not after Christ.

Proverbs 30:5, 6 — Every word of God *is* pure: he *is* a shield unto them that put their trust in him. Add thou not unto his words, lest he reprove thee, and thou be found a liar.

Revelation 22:18 — For I testify unto every man that heareth the words of the prophecy of this book, If any man shall add unto these things, God shall add unto him the plagues that are written in this book...

C.   It makes the apostle Peter the foundation of the church and thus destroys the only true foundation which is laid in Zion.

1 Corinthians 3:11 — For other foundation can no man lay than that is laid, which is Jesus Christ.

Acts 4:12 — Neither is there salvation in any other: for there is none other name under heaven given among men, whereby we must be saved.

D.   It teaches that the pope of Rome is the visible and supreme head of the universal church, and thus denies the fundamental doctrines of the headship and supremacy of Christ.

Ephesians 1:22 — And hath put all *things* under his feet, and gave him *to be* the head over all *things* to the church...

Colossians 1:18 — And he is the head of the body, the church: who is the beginning, the firstborn from the dead; that in all *things* he might have the preeminence.

E.   It conducts the prayers of the church in an unknown tongue, so that they cannot be profitable to the people.

1 Corinthians 14:9, 11, 14, 19 — So likewise ye, except ye utter by the tongue words easy to be understood, how shall it be known what is spoken? for ye shall speak into the air... Therefore if I know not the meaning of the voice, I shall be unto him that speaketh a barbarian, and he that speaketh *shall be* a barbarian unto me... For if I pray in an *unknown* tongue, my spirit prayeth, but my understanding is unfruitful... Yet in the church I had rather speak five words with my understanding, that *by my voice* I might teach others also, than ten thousand words in an *unknown* tongue.

F.   It pays divine worship to the virgin Mary, which is idolatry.

Matthew 4:10 — Then saith Jesus unto him, Get thee hence, Satan: for it is written, Thou shalt worship the Lord thy God, and him only shalt thou serve.

Philippians 2:9-11 — Wherefore God also hath highly exalted him, and given him a name which is above every name: That at the name of Jesus every knee should bow, of *things* in heaven, and *things* in earth, and *things* under the earth;

And *that* every tongue should confess that Jesus Christ *is* Lord, to the glory of God the Father.

G. **It teaches its members to pray to saints and angels as mediators or intercessors while there is, as Scripture teaches, but one mediator between God and man.**

> **Revelation 19:10** — And I fell at his feet to worship him. And he said unto me, See *thou do it* not: I am thy fellowservant, and of thy brethren that have the testimony of Jesus: worship God: for the testimony of Jesus is the spirit of prophecy.
> **1 John 2:1** — My little children, these things write I unto you, that ye sin not. And if any man sin, we have an advocate with the Father, Jesus Christ the righteous...
> **1 Timothy 2:5** — For *there is* one God, and one mediator between God and men, the man Christ Jesus...
> **1 Corinthians 8:6** — But to us *there is but* one God, the Father, of whom *are* all things, and we in him; and one Lord Jesus Christ, by whom *are* all things, and we by him.

H. **It uses images in worship and pays adoration to the sacramental elements, and the images of saints, which is also idolatry.**

> **Exodus 20:4, 5** — Thou shalt not make unto thee any graven image, or any likeness *of any thing* that *is* in heaven above, or that *is* in the earth beneath, or that *is* in the water under the earth: Thou shalt not bow down thyself to them, nor serve them: for I the LORD thy God *am* a jealous God, visiting the iniquity of the fathers upon the children unto the third and fourth *generation* of them that hate me...

I. **It teaches the doctrine of transubstantiation,[99] which is at once absurd and idolatrous.**

> **1 Corinthians 11:26, 28** — For as often as ye eat this bread, and drink this cup, ye do shew the Lord's death till he come... But let a man examine himself, and so let him eat of *that* bread, and drink of *that* cup.

J. **It teaches the doctrine of purgatory,[100] which is pagan in its origin, debasing in its tendency, and contrary to the express teaching of Scripture.**

> **1 John 1:7** — But if we walk in the light, as he is in the light, we have fellowship one with another, and the blood of Jesus Christ his Son cleanseth us from all sin.
> **2 Corinthians 5:2** — For in this we groan, earnestly desiring to be clothed upon with our house which is from heaven...
> **Philippians 1:23** — For I am in a strait betwixt two, having a desire to depart, and to be with Christ; which is far better:
> **Revelation 14:13** — And I heard a voice from heaven saying unto me, Write, Blessed *are* the dead which die in the Lord from henceforth: Yea, saith the Spirit, that they may rest from their labours; and their works do follow them.

K. **It teaches the superstitious observance of times and places.**

L. **It enjoins self-righteous penances.[101]**

---

[99] The doctrine holding that the bread and wine of the Mass are really transformed into the body and blood of Jesus, although their appearances remain the same. [Ed.]

[100] The Roman Catholic invention of a state in which the souls of those who have died in grace must expiate (make amends for) their sins. [Ed.]

[101] A Roman Catholic sacrament that includes contrition, confession to a priest, acceptance of punishment, and absolution. Upon completion of this, there is said to be reconciliation with God. Protestant churches teach that a reconciliation based upon this is works instead of grace. [Ed.]

M.   It assumes the power of granting dispensations[102] and indul-
gences,[103] which is to put itself in the place of God.

N.   In direct opposition to Scripture, it teaches the necessity and
virtue of the celibacy[104] of the clergy.

Against these, and many other errors of the church of Rome, the
Presbyterian church, in common with all the reformed churches,
bears its testimony that they are antichristian and, in their tendency,
destructive to the souls of men.

297.   *By what title should this church be always spoken of?*

Either as the Romish, or the Roman catholic church, or the church
of the pope, that is, the popish church.

298.   *Why should you never speak of that church as the "Catholic church"?*

Because, as has been shown, the term *catholic*, both as it means *universal*, and as it means *orthodox*, applies to all true churches, and not
to any one particular communion, such as the Roman, or Anglican.[105]

299.   *Do you, then, consider the application of the term "catholic" to the
Romish church to be positively wrong?*

I do, for several reasons.
1. Such a use of the term is in itself absurd.
2. It is no distinction, as thus used, any more than the term Christian would be, since it applies equally to other churches.
3. It is unjust as it regards ourselves; for when we call the Roman
the catholic church, it is implied that we ourselves, and all other
churches, are heretics or schismatics.
4. It is uncharitable towards them, since it encourages them in their
error, and affords to them a plausible argument against other
denominations.[106]

---

[102] An exemption from a church law, a vow, or another similar obligation granted in a particular case
by a Roman Catholic official. [Ed.].

[103] The remission of temporal punishment still due for a sin that has been sacramentally absolved.
These have often been sold in order to raise money for the Roman church. The practice of this
was particularly odious to the Reformers. [Ed.]

[104] Remaining unmarried. Cf. 1 Timothy 4:3 [Ed.].

[105] Anglican is the term applied in England to the Episcopal church or Church of England. [Ed.]

[106] The use which they make of it, when it is conceded to them, cannot be unknown. Dr. Milner, in
his *End of Religious Controversy*, (Letter xxv.) says of the (Episcopal) church: *Every time they
address the God of truth, either in solemn worship or in private devotion, they are forced, each of
them, to repeat, I believe in the catholic church; and yet, if I ask any of them the question, are you
a catholic? he is sure to answer me, "No, I am a Protestant!"* Was there ever a more glaring
instance of inconsistency, and self-condemnation, among rational beings? See Whateley's
Romish Errors, p. 331. Let us then, avoid this inconsistency and self-condemnation.

300.   In what sense may the Romish church be called a true church?

The Romish church may be admitted to be a true church inasmuch as it is a *real,* not a fictitious church; but it cannot be allowed to be a true church, in that sense of the word *true,* which would imply that it teaches true doctrines, or is conformed to the order and discipline laid down in the word of God.   In this sense the Romish is not only not the true church, but has no claim to the character of a true church at all.[107]

Section 2
Of prelacy.

301.   What opinion is to be entertained of those churches which, with an orthodox creed, have adopted the prelatic form of church government?

They are to be regarded as churches of Christ; and yet as not being, in their constitution and order, in full accord with the word of God; and therefore imperfect.

302.   Why do you denominate theirs the prelatic, rather than the Episcopal form of church government?

For the same reasons, in part, why we refuse to speak of the Romish, as the catholic church; and, also, because we believe our form of church government to be more truly the primitive and apostolical episcopacy, since the term bishop (that is *episcopos,* whence episcopacy) was, by the Holy Spirit, originally given to presbyters, and is applied to them throughout the New Testament. (See Question 92.)[108]

303.   Do you, then, design to convey any reproach by using the terms prelate, prelacy, and prelatic, instead of bishop, episcopacy, and Episcopal, as applied to this denomination of Christians?

Certainly not, since, in so doing, we use terms which are constantly employed by their own writers in a good sense; and by which this denomination may be distinguished from others.

304.   Can you name some of the points in this prelatic system, to which Presbyterians object, as being without support in the word of God?

A.   Presbyterians object to the power claimed by prelatic churches to decree rites and ceremonies in the worship of God and to institute offices in the church; Christ, alone, as King and Head of the church having any such authority.

Proverbs 30:6 — Add thou not unto his words, lest he reprove thee, and thou be found a liar.   *(cont'd)*

---

[107] See Whateley's *Logic,* Appendix, Art. *Truth,* p. 381, Eng. edition.

[108] Since the writing of this catechism, there have been some prelatic groups formed that have reorganized their form of church government to become more presbyterial, though not fully so. [Ed.]

Revelation 22:18 — For I testify unto every man that heareth the words of the prophecy of this book, If any man shall add unto these things, God shall add unto him the plagues that are written in this book...
1 Corinthians 6:12 — All things are lawful unto me, but all things are not expedient: all things are lawful for me, but I will not be brought under the power of any.
See also Psalm 2:6; 1 Peter 5:3; Ephesians 5:23; Matthew 28:20.

B. **While Presbyterians do not deny the propriety, or reject the use, of all forms of prayer, or of administering ordinances, they object to the imposition of a fixed and stated liturgy, which excludes all extemporaneous prayer; believing that it [i.e., a fixed and stated liturgy] tends to prevent the exercise of spiritual gifts; to induce formality and deadness in devotion; and to prevent its adaptation to the state and circumstances of the church and of individuals.**[109]

Acts 1:24, 25 — And they prayed, and said, Thou, Lord, which knowest the hearts of all *men*, shew whether of these two thou hast chosen, That he may take part of this ministry and apostleship, from which Judas by transgression fell, that he might go to his own place.

C. **Presbyterians object to the appointment and stated observance of holy days as being not only without scriptural warrant, but positively discountenanced by it; as interfering with the due sanctification of the Lord's day; and having originated in improper motives; and as necessarily leading to many and great evils.**

See Galatians 4:9-11.

D. **Presbyterians object to the interposition, in baptism, of godfathers and godmothers between parents and their children. For this practice there is not a shadow of evidence in the New Testament, nor in the practice of the church, for five hundred years after Christ. It was unknown, also, among the Waldenses,**[110] **and is to be regarded as one of the many superstitious usages introduced into the church with the progress of corruption.**

E. **Presbyterians object, for the same reasons, to the use of the sign of the cross in baptism and also because it is associated with superstition and idolatry of the Romish church, in which it is considered as essential to the validity of the ordinance of**

---

[109] *The Book of Common Order of the English Church at Geneva*, drawn up by Knox, and approved by Calvin, was received, and approved, by the Church of Scotland, and ordinarily prefixed to the Psalms in metre. Neither has the use of the truly excellent and beautiful order ever been proscribed, or forbidden; and its use, in a modified form, might be still advantageous. Like the liturgies of all the French Presbyterian churches, it is not exclusive, but provides for the introduction of extemporaneous prayer, and for modifications. Its use has been lately recommended, in an edition by the Rev. J. Cumming, of the Scotch church in London. Our church also allows of forms for profession, baptism and marriage. [By contrast, Presbyterians oppose that which is universally rigid and allows for little or no flexibility in the order of worship. Ed.]

[110] A sect of Christian dissenters that originated in southern France in the late twelfth century and adopted Calvinist doctrines in the sixteenth century. [Ed.]

baptism, is applied in every step of religious life, and is formally and publicly reverenced.

F.   Presbyterians object to the rite of confirmation because they can find no authority for it in the word of God or in the purest ages of the church; because it is altogether superfluous and answers no practical purpose not otherwise provided for; because they regard the form of its administration as teaching dangerous and unscriptural doctrine; and because it serves to foster, in the minds of the young, the most delusive and self-righteous hopes.

G.   Presbyterians object to the practice of kneeling at the Lord's supper, because it is contrary to the posture assumed by Christ and his apostles, who employed that posture in which it was then customary to receive ordinary meals; because it was unknown in the Christian church for a number of centuries; because it is opposed to that gladness, gratitude, and affectionate intercourse of which this ordinance is expressive; because it is a remnant of the Romish ritual and of the adoration of the host; and because it was retained in the English church against the wishes of a large body of its most learned and pious divines.

H.   Presbyterians object to the *regular* administration of the Lord's supper in private, as opposed to the social character of this ordinance; as being unwarranted by Scripture; as fostering superstitious notions of the inherent virtues of the sacrament; as liable to great and manifold abuses; and as likely to do much injury to many, both among the living and the dying.

I.   Presbyterians object to bowing in the public service at the name of Jesus. This also is without any authority from Scripture. It attaches some superstitious virtue to one, among many other titles, of our blessed Redeemer. It seems to imply that the second person of the ever-glorious Trinity is entitled to peculiar adoration. And as it was first introduced about the fifteenth century, it should not be retained among a reformed Christian people.

J.   Presbyterians object, for similar reasons, to the practice of praying toward the east; of wearing, in the reading-desk or during the prayers, a white surplice; of speaking of the Lord's table as an altar, of the Lord's supper as a sacrifice, and of Christian ministers as priests; these terms being pagan in their origin, Jewish in their spirit, and the last being at variance with the whole system of the Gospel and destructive of one of its most important characteristics.

K.   Presbyterians also solemnly protest against reading the apocryphal books in any service regarded as connected with the worship of God, which is done continually in prelatic churches on their holy days. These books form no part of the inspired word of God; they contain false doctrines, misstatements, and not a few things adapted to promote ridicule, rather than edification; and are acknowledged by prelatists themselves to be uncanonical,[111] and very exceptionable in much that they contain.[112]

305. *As some of these ceremonies appear unimportant in themselves, why is the observance of them a ground of serious objection?*

Because such observance encourages superstition and *will-worship*; is opposed to the sufficiency of the Scriptures as the only rule of faith and practice, and to that liberty wherewith Christ has made us free; and upholds the unscriptural and pernicious principle that men may innocently and profitably add to the institutions of Christ and the terms of communion in his church, these ceremonies being regarded as mystical and significant.

Colossians 2:20, 23; Galatians 5:1.

306. *Is there any thing else in the prelacy to which Presbyterians object?*

Yes; they object to the power of ordination, and other ecclesiastical functions, being vested exclusively in the unscriptural order of prelates, since this makes void the word of God, and leads to spiritual despotism.

1 Timothy 4:14 — Neglect not the gift that is in thee, which was given thee by prophecy, with the laying on of the hands of the presbytery.
Matthew 20:25, 27 — But Jesus called them *unto him*, and said, Ye know that the princes of the Gentiles exercise dominion over them, and they that are great exercise authority upon them... And whosoever will be chief among you, let him be your servant...

Again; they object to the unscriptural distinction between consecration, or the setting apart of prelates, and ordination, or the setting apart of presbyters, to the work of the Gospel ministry, as being wholly unauthorized by the word of God.

Further; they object to the doctrine that, by water-baptism, an infant is regenerated, made a member of Christ, and a child of God; and various other things contained in the canons authorized by this church and in the *Book of Common Prayer*.

James 1:18 — Of his own will begat he us with the word of truth, that we should be a kind of firstfruits of his creatures. *(cont'd)*

---

[111] Contrary to the canon of Scripture. [Ed.]

[112] The Church of England omits the public reading of two hundred and eleven chapters of the Bible, and substitutes one hundred and one chapters from the Apocrypha. The Homilies speak of Baruch as a prophet, and expressly ascribes the book of *Tobit* to the Holy Spirit. See *Homily Against Disobedience and Rebellion*, Part. i .p. 475., and on Almsdeed, Part. ii. p. 328. These homilies make a part of the formularies of the Episcopal church in this country. For a full exhibition of the grounds of our objection to these ceremonies, see Dr. Samuel Miller on *Presbyterianism*, etc. ch. v. p. 63, etc.

1 Peter 1:23 — Being born again, not of corruptible seed, but of incorruptible, by the word of God, which liveth and abideth for ever.

Finally, they lament the extreme laxity of many of the prelatical churches in reference to the characters whom they admit to their communion and privileges, and the difficulties thrown in the way of any of their godly ministers attempting to exercise a scriptural discipline.

Section 3
Of congregationalism.

307. *In what light do Presbyterians regard those churches which adopt the independent or congregational form of church government?*[113]

As far as they hold to those doctrines which are regarded by the Presbyterian church as the doctrines of grace, we consider them also to be true churches of Jesus Christ; but as defective, and not *fully* accordant to Scripture in their forms of government and discipline.

308. *Name some of the reasons why Presbyterians object to this system of church government.*

A.   Presbyterians object to it because, so far as it makes each congregation independent of every other, it destroys the unity and power of the church.

> **1 Corinthians 12:12, 26, 27** — For as the body is one, and hath many members, and all the members of that one body, being many, are one body: so also *is* Christ... And whether one member suffer, all the members suffer with it; or one member be honoured, all the members rejoice with it. Now ye are the body of Christ, and members in particular.
> **John 18:36** — Jesus answered, My kingdom is not of this world: if my kingdom were of this world, then would my servants fight, that I should not be delivered to the Jews: but now is my kingdom not from hence.

B.   Presbyterians object to it because it is thus opposed to the constitution of the apostolic church in which there existed ecclesiastical courts, as bonds of union between the churches. (See Chapter 4)

C.   Presbyterians object to it because it destroys the original distinction recognized in Scripture between the rulers or officers, and the members of the church.

> **Hebrews 13:17, 24** — Obey them that have the rule over you, and submit yourselves: for they watch for your souls, as they that must give account, that they may do it with joy, and not with grief: for that *is* unprofitable for you... Salute all them that have the rule over you, and all the saints. They of Italy salute you.

---

[113] The reader should be apprised that, in this place, congregationalism is considered, in its theoretic and essential principles, as a system. In its practical operation in this country, it is found acting upon those principles of consociation [close association] and union, both in ecclesiastical and benevolent matters, which gives such unity and strength to the Presbyterian church, and is, therefore, essentially Presbyterian.

D. **Presbyterians object to it because it unfits[114] the church, in her distinctive character and through her own organization, to perform her appropriate duty of extending the kingdom of Christ throughout the world.[115]**

Matthew 18:19, 20 — Again I say unto you, That if two of you shall agree on earth as touching any thing that they shall ask, it shall be done for them of my Father which is in heaven. For where two or three are gathered together in my name, there am I in the midst of them.

E. **Presbyterians object to it because it gives an unrestricted, and therefore unscriptural, power to its members in the government of the church.** (See Chapter 3.)

F. **Presbyterians object to it because it deprives the pastor, or any aggrieved member of the church, of the privilege of appealing to some court of review.**

Acts 15:2 — When therefore Paul and Barnabas had no small dissension and disputation with them, they determined that Paul and Barnabas, and certain other of them, should go up to Jerusalem unto the apostles and elders about this question.

Section 4
Of the doctrine of the apostolical succession.

309. *To what other doctrine, common to both Romanists and prelatists, do you object?*

To their doctrine of the apostolical succession.

310. *Is it not important that there should be a regular succession of scripturally appointed ministers?*

It is important as a matter of order but it is not essential to the salvation of souls, since a broken succession can never frustrate the efficacy of the divine word, or an unbroken succession sanctify *the doctrines of demons,* or the *works of darkness.*[116]

See 1 Timothy 4:1; Romans 13:12; Ephesians 5:11

311. *Are there any who believe in the absolute necessity, in order to [have a] covenanted salvation, of such a succession?*[117]

Yes, the popish church, and a large party [number] in the Episcopal churches of America and of England.

---

[114] Makes the church less capable and tending towards unfitness. [Ed.]

[115] The church needs teamwork, cooperation, and discipline in the extending of the kingdom. This is not the history of the Congregationalist churches and therefore has been detrimental (*unfits the church*) to worldwide task. [Ed.]

[116] The Roman church has put such an emphasis on its supposed apostolic succession while ignoring the teachings of the *doctrines of devils [demons]* and *works of darkness* by its leaders. [Ed.]

[117] The essence of this question in modern day language is: *Do any believe that you have to be in a church with apostolic succession to be saved?* [Ed.]

312.   **What is meant by this doctrine of apostolical succession?**

By the prelatical doctrine of apostolical succession, it is taught, that as Christ delegated all power to his apostles, so have these apostles delegated it to the order of prelates in personal and perpetual succession; that these prelates are the sources of all spiritual grace and authority; are alone empowered to ordain other ministers so that without them there can be no valid ministry at all; that they alone possess or can bestow the gifts of the Holy Spirit; and that without them, all preaching and ordinances are vain, delusive, and deprived of the promised blessing of Christ.[118]

313.   **Can this doctrine be proved from Scripture?**

No; it is not even pretended that this doctrine can be found in Scripture. It is granted, that it is not clearly revealed in the word of God; but that it depends upon tradition and the authority of the fathers.[119] This doctrine, on the contrary, is actually denounced by Christ; and is opposed to Scripture declarations, warnings, and precepts, to its promises and prophecies, to its facts and decisions, and to the only remaining commission of the ministry.[120]

Mark 10:42, 43; and 9:33-37. Matthew 23:8-11.

314.   **Can this personal succession be shown to have been preserved in a valid and unbroken chain?**

In order to show this, it must be proved that the ordination of every prelate in the entire succession was valid, first, as to the form of ordination; secondly, as to the subject of ordination; and, thirdly, as to the ministers of ordination, which is an impossibility.[121]

315.   **Can this personal succession be proved as a historical fact?**

On the contrary, it cannot be proved that the apostle Peter, the first link in this chain, was ever at Rome, or that he was ever bishop of Rome, or that he ever appointed a successor to himself, as such. Neither can it be decided whether there were one or two bishops originally at Rome, nor who were the first successors in that church; while it is certain that many invalidities[122] have occurred in the progress of this succession, in its Romish, Anglican, and American branches, and also in all the other prelatic churches; and that it has been broken in numerous instances, and in innumerable ways.[123]

---

[118] See the author's *Lectures on the Prelatical Doctrine of the Apostolical Succession.*

[119] See full proof of this position in author's *Lectures*, pp. 73, 83, 87, 99, 103, 133, 134, 136.

[120] See Ibid. lect. vi. and vii.

[121] See Ibid. lect. v.

[122] claims without foundation in truth [Ed.]

[123] See Ibid. lect. viii. and ix.

316. *Are prelates really and in fact successors of the apostles?*

Prelates are not successors to the apostles, in fact. They are not apostles in the true sense of this title, which was limited to the twelve; nor in their call, which was immediately from Christ; nor in their endowments for their office, which were supernatural; nor in their office itself, which was the oversight and instruction of the whole world; nor in their duties, which involved the indoctrination, care, and government of ALL the churches.[124]

317. *Can this doctrine be sustained on the ground of reason?*

No; it is most unreasonable, inasmuch as it substitutes the theory of man for the word of God; the visible organization and ministry of the church, for spiritual Christianity; ordinances, rites, and forms, for doctrines and inward graces; the authority of the church, for the supremacy and headship of Christ; and the means of attaining salvation, by giving efficacy to the truth, for that salvation itself.[125]

318. *Does this doctrine necessarily lead to popery?*

This doctrine necessarily leads to popery because it invests the church with all authority; because it subjugates the laity and ministry to prelates; because it consigns to these prelates the interpretation of the word of God; because it has ever formed the basis upon which the system of popery rests its exclusive assumptions; because, wherever it has been carried out, it has led to the introduction of the corrupt doctrines and practices of the Romish church; and because it is now leading extensively to the same results.[126]

319. *Is this doctrine also intolerant in its tendencies and results?*

That this doctrine leads to intolerance in spirit and in practice is proved from its history in all past ages; from the character and doings of many ancient and modern prelates; from its necessary tendency to exclude the laity from all ecclesiastical jurisdiction, to consolidate a spiritual despotism, and to claim absolute authority over the persons, conduct, and opinions of its adherents; from its bitter, sectarian, and uncharitable spirit towards all other denominations; and from its clear opposition to civil and religious liberty.[127]

320. *What further objection have you to this doctrine of apostolical succession?*

I object to it because it necessarily implies that the church of Rome is truly catholic, apostolical, and indefectible[128] in doctrine and practice, and that all other churches, being excommunicated by it, are cut off

---

[124] See Ibid. lect. x.

[125] See Ibid. lect. xiv.

[126] See Ibid. lect. xi. and xii.

[127] See Ibid. lect. xiii.

[128] not capable of error [Ed.]

from the church of Christ; and because it is schismatical, leading its abettors, like the ancient heretics, to cut themselves off from all other Christians, to assert that they alone constitute THE catholic church of Christ, and to deny to all other branches of the church either a valid ministry or efficacious[129] ordinances; and because it is thus contradictory to the charity, to the spirituality, and to the divine character of the Gospel. [130]

321. *Is this doctrine to be rejected because such claims might be advanced only by prelatists?*

On the contrary, Presbyterians might far more reasonably urge these claims. For as all their ministers are bishops; as their bishops, at the reformation, were ordained by those in authority; as they can undeniably trace their succession upward through the Romish, the Waldensian, and the Culdee churches, to the very time of the apostles; and as in their time bishops were presbyters, and acted under the one and only commission given by divine appointment; it is therefore plain, that while their ministerial succession is certain and unquestionable, that of prelates never can be established.

322. *Why, then, are we not to glory in this succession?*

Because they only are true bishops of Jesus Christ, who are called of God; who receive his Spirit; and who preach his truth in its purity and its fullness; this being the all-essential mark of the church of Christ.[131]

323. *What evils arise from the assertion, that this unbroken succession of prelates is essential to a true church, to a true ministry, and to all hope of covenanted mercy?*

This doctrine would destroy all existing churches, and thus, all hope of salvation; since there is no church which can establish such a succession. It also fosters pride and ambition among the clergy; lukewarmness, formality, and hypocrisy among the laity; and carnality, contention, and animosity among all Protestant denominations. It strengthens popery by conceding its essential principles and its most arrogant demands. And it strengthens infidelity, by implicating Christianity in a doctrine which is in itself unscriptural, in its tendency hurtful, in its evidence baseless, and in its reasoning absurd.

---

[129] produces the intended results [Ed.]

[130] See Ibid. lect. xv. xvii. xviii. and xix.

[131] See Ibid. lect. xx., and xxi.

Section 5
The advantages and claims of the Presbyterian church.

324. *What claims, then, has the Presbyterian church on all her members?*

She is scriptural in her character, ordinances, and doctrines; apostolic in her forms, officers, and order of government and worship; adapted to secure the religious liberty and prosperity of all her members, and to extend the blessings of salvation to the ends of the earth.

325. *What other advantages does the Presbyterian church possess, to recommend her to all her members?*

In her government there is found ample provision, according to the word of God, for the preservation of order, free from all confusion; of peace and unity, free from schism and division; of the truth as it is in Jesus, free from all error and heresy; of piety, free from all scandal and profaneness; of equity and right, free from all maladministration, whether ignorant, arbitrary, or tyrannical; of the honor and purity of Christ's ordinances, free from all contempt, pollution, and profanation; of the comfort, quickening, and encouragement of the saints in all the ways of Christ; and of the honor of God and of our Lord Jesus, in all the services of the sanctuary.

326. *Name some of the further advantages possessed by members of the Presbyterian church?*

They possess the right of choosing their own pastors and elders; they are neither subject to the spiritual despotism of a priesthood, nor to anarchy and misrule; they can bring any matter, — whether it be unfaithfulness in ministers and elders, or in the other officers and members of the church, or errors in doctrine, — before the church courts, composed of an equal proportion of clergymen and of representatives of the people, chosen by themselves, for investigation and decision; and they have the privilege and power, when their rights as citizens of Zion are assailed, of appealing from one church court to another.

327. *Are not the principles of Presbyterian polity in perfect agreement with the principles of civil liberty?*

Yes; in the equality of all her members and ministers; in her love of simplicity and order; in her opposition to all unnecessary distinction; in her regard to the interests and wishes of her members as well as ministers; in the open publicity of all her doings; in that model she has given for the exercise of the principle of representation; in that shield which she has thrown around the person and character of the poorest of her members; in that energy with which her various enterprises are carried on; in a word, in her perfect unity combined with diffusiveness[132] and universality, she exhibits all the principles and features of true liberty, whether civil or ecclesiastical.

Matthew 28:19, 20 — Go ye therefore, and teach all nations, baptizing them in the name of the Father, and of the Son, and of the Holy Ghost: Teaching them to observe all things whatsoever I have commanded you: and, lo, I am with you alway, *even* unto the end of the world. Amen.

328. *What is the duty of members of the Presbyterian church toward members of other Christian churches?*

They should respect their religious opinions and practices; avoid all bigotry and prejudice; abstain from all officious[133] controversy, and underhand proselytism; reciprocate all acts of Christian courtesy and kind regard; and cooperate with them in the promotion of every good word and work.

329. *What, then, is the claim which the Presbyterian church makes upon the regards of all her members?*

She claims to be regarded as a true and pure church, having the pure word preached, and the sacraments duly administered; and as an entire and perfect church, having that apostolic form, order, and ministry, which can be traced back to Christ and his apostles. But while her discipline is the best, she does not wish it to be regarded as the *only* form of church government that gives validity to ordinances or hope of salvation.

Section 6
Of the relation of the Presbyterian church to the world.

330. *In what relation does the church stand to the world*

Christ has appointed his church to be the salt of the earth, that it may be preserved from premature destruction; to be the pillar and ground[134] of the truth; and to be a missionary association to send forth teachers and gather all nations unto Christ.

Matthew 5:13; 1 Timothy 3:15; Matthew 28:19.

331. *What is the duty of the church as the salt of the earth?*

As the earth is preserved only for the sake of the church, it is the duty of the church carefully to retain its purity and to show a good example to all around; lest, having lost its savor, the judgments of God should come upon the world.

Matthew 24:22; 5:13, as above.

---

[132] spreading influence [Ed.]

[133] *i.e.,* with excessive eagerness [Ed.].

[134] support and foundation [Ed.]

332. *What is the duty of the church as the ground of the truth?*

It is the duty of the church, as the ground of the truth, to preserve and circulate the Scriptures, pure and entire; earnestly to contend for the faith once delivered to the saints; and to adorn the doctrine of Christ by exhibiting in its members a walk and conversation becoming the Gospel that others, seeing their good works, may be led to glorify their Father who is in heaven.

2 Timothy 2:2; Jude 3; Titus 2:10; Matthew 5:16.

333. *What is the duty of the church to the world as the pillar of the truth?*[135]

It is the duty of the church, as the pillar of the truth, to consider herself as a missionary association organized by Christ for the promotion of God's glory in the evangelization of the world.

Romans 12:5-8; Revelation 22:17; Galatians 4:18; 2 Corinthians 12:15; Acts ch. 13 and 15.

334. *What has Christ promised with regard to the future destiny of the church?*

Christ has promised that all countries shall yet be filled with the knowledge of the Lord; and that with the ingathering of the Gentiles, the Jews shall be restored to their forfeited privileges and made full partakers of all the blessings of the Gospel.

Romans 11:25-27; Matthew 28:19.

335. *What influence is the church fitted to exert upon the state of the world?*

As all misery sprung originally from sin, so is it maintained only by its continuance. And thus, when Christianity shall be extended over the whole world, poverty and disease will be greatly decreased, while that which remains will be softened by the exercise of faith in God and the sympathy of our fellowmen — the happiness and prosperity of individuals will be increased by the restoration of communion with God and obtaining his blessing according to his promise, the faithful performance of the duties which men owe to each other, and promotion of truth, peace, and love among all men; the resources of nations will be increased and their expenditures diminished; and the general happiness of mankind will be promoted by the acquisition and enjoyment of health and wealth, the diffusion of industry, temperance, and morality, by providing conscientious servants, neighbors, and friends, and by establishing confidence, and diffusing intelligence, kindness, respect, meekness, and prudence among all ranks and classes of society.

Ephesians 5:6; Isaiah 32:15-18; Revelation 3:20; Job 36:11; Romans 13:7-10; Luke 2:14; James 2:15; Psalm 117:17; Proverbs 15:6; Ephesians 6:3; 1 Thessalonians 4:11, 12; Matthew 5:5, 9; Proverbs 14:34.

---

[135] The reference is to pillars as anciently used for proclaiming to the world and to future times the knowledge of great events.

336. *Why, then, is it the especial and imperative duty of the Presbyterian church, and of every member of it, to engage with all their powers in the great work of spreading the Gospel throughout the earth?*

Since it is thus the great end and duty of the church to act as a missionary association, this also must be the great end and duty of the Presbyterian church, as a branch of the Catholic church; and since the purest form of Christianity, which derives all its doctrines, polity, and worship from the pure word of God, to labor earnestly for its extension to the ends of the earth.

Biographical Information on Thomas Smyth

Thomas Smyth (1808-1873) was born in Belfast, Northern Ireland where he spent his youth. He began his higher education at Belfast College (1827-1829). In 1829, he entered Highbury College in London, where he studied in the classics and theology completing his education at Princeton Seminary in United States in 1831. He was ordained in 1831 and labored for forty years as the pastor of Second Presbyterian Church in Charleston, South Carolina. From his research in his own extensive library (said to be one of the largest private collections in the United States at the time) he wrote several massive volumes on church officers. His love of scholarship persuaded him to leave an endowment for the Smyth Lectureship at Columbia Theological Seminary. He was a scholarly pastor and an Old School Presbyterian. He ardently supported the cause of the Confederate States of America and survived the War Between the States by some years. His study and experience combined to lead him to the belief that confusion in the offices creates strife in the church. The goal of his writing was to clearly define and distinguish the offices and functions continuing in the church.

Dr. Smyth is little known today. Those who have heard of him, may have read his "Argument for Church-Boards" in *The Collected Writings of James Henley Thornwell*, Vol. 4, Appendix A. However, his articles written for *The Biblical Repertory and Princeton Review* and *North Carolina Presbyterian* compiled in *Theories of the Eldership* are still a relatively unknown refutation of the views of ruling eldership commonly known today as the "two-office" view in the United States. The editor of the North Carolina Presbyterian, had this to say about his *Theories*, *"Dr. Robt. L. Dabney, to whom they were mainly addressed, was then Professor in Union Theological Seminary, Virginia. Drs. J. H. Thornwell and John B. Adger, frequently mentioned in the discussion, were Professors in the Columbia Theological Seminary. Drs. Smyth and Adger were brothers-in-law. The debate in the Southern church on these subjects continuing until about 1878, was a battle between giants. Dr. Smyth was the leader on one side. He showed himself a skillful warrior, mighty and well-armed. Many believe that though the votes were finally against him, he won the victory on the field of truth and history for the theory he defended."* His position was to maintain the view of eldership found in the *Form of Government* from the Westminster Assembly. He viewed the others as a departure.

Dr. Thomas Smyth was also the author of *Lectures on the Apostolical Succession; Presbytery and not Prelacy, the Scriptural and Primitive Polity; Ecclesiastical Republicanism* and many other items in his ten volume *Complete Works* collected posthumously (1908-1912).

Suggested Bibliography

On Presbyterian Government In General:

James Bannerman — *The Church of Christ, Edinburgh,* Banner of Truth, 1960
Mark R. Brown — *Order in the Offices*
    The Essence of Presbyterianism
John Calvin — *The Institutes of the Christian Religion (Vol. 2, Book 4)*
David W. Hall & Joseph H. Hall — *Paradigms of Polity*
G. D. Henderson — *Presbyterianism*
    Why We Are Presbyterians
Charles Hodge — *Selections from Church Polity*
J. A. Hodge — *What is Presbyterian Law?*
B. Kuiper — *The Glorious Body of Christ*
Samuel Miller — *Presbyterianism — The Truly Primitive and Apostolical Constitution of the Church of Christ*
London Ministers — *Jus Divinum Regiminis Ecclesiastici The Divine Right of Church Government*
James Henley Thornwell — *Collected Writings, Vol. IV*

On Ministers of the Word

James L. Ainslie — *The Doctrines of Ministerial Order in the Reformed Churches of the 16th and 17th Centuries*
Edmund P. Clowney — *Called to the Ministry*
    Living in Christ's Church
    The Relations of Ministers to Ruling Elders
Paul E. G. Cook — *Preaching — A Divine Calling*
    The Minister and the Church — Biblical Attitudes
Leonard Coppes — *Who Will Lead Us*
Harry G. Goodykoontz — *The Minister in the Reformed Tradition*
David T. Gordon — *Equipping Ministry in Ephesians 4?*
Robert W. Henderson — *The Teaching Office in the Reformed Tradition*
Martin Lloyd-Jones — *Preaching and Preachers*
Pierre Ch. Marcel — *The Relevance of Preaching*
Geoffrey Thomas — *The Pastoral Ministry*

On Ruling Elders

Mark R. Brown — *Qualifications for Ruling Elders*
Peter Colin Campbell — *The Theory of Ruling Eldership*
David Dickson — *The Elder and His Work*
G. D. Henderson — *The Scottish Ruling Elder*
Charles Hodge — *The Warrant for Ruling Elders*
J. Aspinwall Hodge — *The Ruling Elder at Work*
Cleland Boyd McAfee — *The Ruling Elder*
Samuel Miller — *The Ruling Elder*
Thomas Smyth — *The Name, Nature, and Function of Ruling Elders*
    Theories of the Eldership I and II

On Deacons

Berghoef and DeKoster — *The Deacon's Handbook*
Andrew Jumper — *Chosen to Serve*
Timothy Keller — *Ministries of Mercy*
Thomas Smyth — *The Office and Functions of Deacons*

www.ingramcontent.com/pod-product-compliance
Lightning Source LLC
LaVergne TN
LVHW091203080426
835509LV00006B/805